TO! Dorothy

AL ways chase The dream
That God has placed in
your heart. AND

Never Give uP.

Robert J Gamon

NEVER GIVE UP

ROBERT J. GANNON, AUTHOR

All scripture contained in Never Give Up is from the New King James Bible (NKJV)

ISBN: 978-0-578-79641-3
Copyright 2020
Published and Printed in the United States

email us at Never Give Up Publishing Company:

nevergiveup.pub.co@gmail.com for information on purchase of **NEVER GIVE UP** books including quantity discounts.

Information is also available for scheduling of speaking events, radio broadcasts, and/or stories for newsletters, magazines, etc.

BATTLEFIELD PRAYER

"God, I'm not asking you to spare my life but to give me the courage to get through this day. If my courage should fail me, please don't let me leave this battlefield alive because I could never face my men, my family, or myself."

Sergeant Robert J. Gannon
United States Marine Corps

Dedicated to Judy Gannon, my wife—
a partner and inspiration always
in my bad times,
my best friend and coworker
in our horse adventures
and in our many other laborious
farming accomplishments.

Judy was also a talented and beautiful
singer and musician who many times
shared her amazing talents and time in
ministry with the VFW and many others.

Judy Gannon 1951-2020

<u>CONTRIBUTORS</u>

Author: Robert J. Gannon

Editor/Business Partner: Linda Galbraith

Editor/Design and Technology: Trish Gannon Rielly

Editor/Photos: Jean Gannon Buersmeyer

Editor/Photos: Joan Gannon Philbert

Editor   Tim Rielly

Editor: Chris Schofield

Editor: Allen Schofield

Editor: James Galbraith

Editor: Sharon Gannon Murphy

Reviewer: Sharon Emmerling

Reviewer: Jackie Gannon Luetkemeyer

Reviewer: Patty Kessinger Black

Reviewer/Technology: Diane Brown

Illustrator: Zarek Galbraith

Illustrator: Dave Garner

TABLE OF CONTENTS

GROWING UP IN ARGYLE

I was born in St. Louis, Missouri, in 1942, the second oldest of five siblings. I was about 7 years old when we moved from St. Louis to Argyle in 1949. Argyle is a small town located in Central Missouri, approximately 30 miles southeast of Jefferson City, Missouri, with a population of about 160. We moved from the city of St. Louis to an old, rundown, two-story farmhouse with no electricity, running water, or indoor plumbing. We did, however, have a cistern, which is a subsurface concrete tank used to store rainwater collected from the roof of the house. When it rained, you had to allow dirt and debris to first be washed from the roof before redirecting the roof drain into the cistern. The cistern didn't hold much water; maybe 200 to 300 gallons. So having access to clean water was always an issue. We went from all of the family each taking a bath every night when we lived in St. Louis to the whole family taking a bath just once a week and having to share the same tub of water. Bath night was normally held on Saturday nights before we went to church on Sunday mornings. If you were the last one in line for your bath, you might come out dirtier than when you went in!

During the winter months, the entire house was heated by one wood stove located on the main floor. The bedrooms were located on the second floor and there were no floor vents to allow any heat to go upstairs. The walls of the house had little or no insulation. On windy days, you could feel the draft blowing through the house, and we had to bury ourselves underneath a huge set of covers. By morning, the wood in the stove would be burned down and would have to be restarted in the morning in order to have heat. During the midwinter months, if you took a glass of water upstairs, the water would be frozen by morning.

A small, wooden outhouse was located probably about 100 to 150 yards from the house. One nightmarish thing was to wake up at 2 o'clock on a cold winter morning and have to go to the bathroom. I dreaded having to make the trip to the outhouse, walking through the dark, cold, scary night to have to sit bare bottom over an open hole and on that **COLD** wooden seat! We were lucky we didn't get stuck to it! In the summertime, I always looked down into that hole before I sat on it, as I was always worried there might be a snake in there ready to bite me!

Moving from a big city was a huge life change for us. We bought several milk cows and chickens; we also raised hogs and beef for butchering. My job started at age 7 years old was to feed the chickens, collect the eggs, and milk the cows. We also raised a hundred or more chickens which we butchered and sold in town. That was always a job we hated—chopping the chickens' heads off and then plunging their bodies into a large pot of boiling water and then hand pluck the feathers off. It was really a bloody, stinking job!

There were no jobs in Argyle. It was a self-contained town and a farming community. It had two feed stores and an MFA elevator where we could buy feed for our animals. There were three taverns in town, and one tavern was a kind of a combination tavern/grocery store where they sold a minimal amount of groceries. Then there was also a hardware/clothing store where we could buy mostly work clothes. But most of the jobs were in Jefferson City, which was about 30 miles away. Ten of those miles were single-lane, rough, gravel road before reaching paved highway, so we didn't go to the city very often. Going to Jefferson City was a big treat! We went there once or twice a year to get school clothes and other supplies not available in Argyle.

Most people in Argyle were poor, but we really didn't know we were poor. A lot of people came to town to get feed and/or groceries on Saturday with their teams of horses or mules pulling wagons. Some of the men would end up in one of the taverns

and become so inebriated that they
unable to drive their teams back h
When this happened, friends would ju
them in the back of their wagon, cu
horses or mules loose, and those t
would just make their way their way
home. We didn't have to worry about d
driving.

Since there really weren't any gr
stores in Argyle, we raised and cannec
canned our own food. In addition to ra
beef, hogs, and chickens to butcher, we
hunted   rabbits,   squirrels   and
whatever we could find to contribute t
family's food supply.

We had a one-acre garden where
grew our vegetables. During the sun
months, we picked wild blackberries
gathered sassafras roots for tea. We h
smokehouse where we cured our
meat. Since we didn't have any typ
refrigeration, all the meat had to be sa
cured and smoked in a smokehouse.

But it was a great place to grow up except for the lack of running water, no heat, the outhouse experiences, killing chickens, getting up to milk the cows at 5 o'clock in the morning in the middle of the winter, cutting firewood with a crosscut saw and an ax, and the ongoing job of pulling weeds, plowing and maintaining a garden. But life got a whole lot better in 1954 when we finally got electricity and a well for running water; best of all, making indoor plumbing accessible.

In Argyle there was little to no crime. We didn't even have any police in town. The town was totally self-policed. People helped one another. If somebody was sick and needed their crops harvested and put up for the season, people would just show up and do it.

One of the unique things about Argyle, like so many other small rural towns, was that there were no bathrooms in any of the stores. There was, however, a community outhouse which was located

right next to the tavern that also sold groceries. It was constructed across a little stream, and the waste from the outhouse dropped directly into the stream below, where the current carried the waste downstream. That was a pretty good system during the winter and spring, but about August, that stream would dry up, and the whole town would stink. Since that was the only bathroom available for people, the waste would pile up until the next rain. We would get a rain which would move everything out, but that stream flowed into a bigger stream which had some fish in it. However, the fish were safe in that stream since nobody ever went fishing downstream or in the small stream which ran into the bigger creek. The bigger creek was called Lewis Creek.

Everybody in Argyle and the surrounding area looked forward to the Saturday night dances. Local people from the area who could play music would get together and form a small band. I don't know if any of them were very good or not, but we didn't know the difference. Square dancing was a big deal as well as the church picnics. The Catholic church had a picnic once a year. They had all kinds of outdoor games and things such as bingo, baked goods for sale, quilt auctions and such. It didn't matter how old you were. They had a beer stand there. If you were 10, 12, 13 years old; if you had a quarter, you could buy a beer.

We walked everywhere, and walking 4 or 5 miles wasn't anything. We would walk that far to somebody's house just to visit. It just was something you had to do. All the roads were rough gravel, so we didn't ride a bicycle too much.

My oldest sister Sharon always enjoyed riding the train that came through town. (I think that's how the town really got started.) As kids, our big entertainment, besides hunting and fishing, would be going to the train station. The guy that ran the train depot had that telegraph, and we would sit there and listen to him type his dots and dashes forever (at least an hour and a half). We thought he was the smartest man in the world. My sister and her girlfriend used to save their money to ride the train for 50 cents to a little town called Belle, Missouri, located about 20 miles to the east. Then the train turned around and would take them back to Argyle. (If it wasn't for Sharon's friend Helen's dad, they would not have gotten on the train. He had to flag the train down for them because it didn't stop in Argyle.)

My twin sisters Jean and Joan have some fond memories of living in Argyle. One of the memories is that Tobey's Circus used to come by once a year. It was set up in a field about a quarter of a mile from our house. The field was owned by Mrs. Hagenhoff. They said they would stay with Mrs. Hagenhoff during the day so they could watch the service workers set up the tent. Tobey's Circus was a big deal. They put on some comedy skits. They also showed a movie such as Hopalong Cassidy, Roy Rogers, etc. Since we had no electricity, movies were a phenomenal treat. A lot of people from the surrounding areas showed up every night. The tent was pretty well packed every night.

When we had company from St. Louis, the girls would go down to the railroad tracks. The people on the train would throw their bottles out the window, and the girls could pick up the bottles. They took them down to the store where they got 2 cents per bottle. They could get Slo-Poke suckers which cost 5 cents. They also helped Mrs. Hagenhoff put flowers on graves on All Souls Day. They were able to pick the flowers from her garden, and they designed the flowers at the crosses.

One of the twins' not-so-good memories was the Sears catalogue in the outhouse.

My sister Jackie, the youngest sibling, remembers working at the fish pond at the Argyle picnic. She enjoyed giving toys to the kids. She said they also picked up beer bottles at the picnic, and when they got a full case, they turned them in for 10 cents.

She remembers that when it snowed, our family enjoyed sledding down the country lane.

Jackie also tells the story of her brother Bob (me) giving her a penny. But she put it in her mouth and swallowed it! We kept checking, but it never passed! She had to have emergency surgery and still has kept the penny to this day.

The phone line we had was like Mayberry (if you watched Mayberry), Argyle had a central phone system, which was called a "party line." The lady that operated the switchboard was named Ida Brandel. On our line there were eight families, and every home had a different ring, but the ringing could be heard on all the phone lines. Your ring could be two longs or a long and a short and so forth. Our ring was two long and one short. But everybody could hear everybody's ring, and since nobody had any televisions or radios, our entertainment sometimes would be listening in on other people's phone calls.

You had to pick up the receiver very quietly and hold your hand over the mouthpiece so no one else could pick up on any background noise.

When my grandma was having a heart attack, she called my mom and said, "Come quick." Everyone on the party line came, most with buckets; they thought my grandma had a fire!

My sister Sharon also always says that the town was caring and friendly, and people were always helpful. When she was just a young kid, she wanted to learn how to crochet. She heard one lady was very good at crocheting. So my sister just went up to her house and asked her if she would teach her how to crochet, and the lady agreed. I think my sister had to buy a few crocheting supplies, go to the lady's house, and the lady taught her how to crochet.

It was just a great place to grow up. Nobody had much. The only thing we really had was each other and the friendship.

People had to help each other in order to survive.

CHILDHOOD PERSONAL LIFE

Some of my life as a child was really good, and some of it was really bad. The good was the town, the people, and my friends. My friends and I went fishing; I loved to fish! We might have to walk 2 or 3 miles to get to some good fishing holes, but we also vigorously hunted. All my friends had squirrel dogs and rabbit dogs; so in our spare time, when there was nothing to do during the wintertime, we hunted rabbits, and in the summertime, we hunted squirrels. That was just great!

Baseball was huge! Back in the 50s, every town had a men's baseball team and a youth boys' team. I played on the youth team. It was very hard to get a team together, let alone practice. Since Argyle was a small, rural farming community, everybody was working quite a bit. We would practice sometimes on Saturdays. So many team members lived outside of town, and had to walk 3 or 4 miles for baseball practice and turn around and walk back home.

One of the best things my friends and I used to do was get together in the wintertime and go gigging or rabbit hunting as a group. Sometimes in the summertime we would have a cookout. We would go squirrel hunting and shoot some squirrels, then we would meet up again at a place on the creek. We almost always had beer. There weren't any policemen in Argyle to check IDs. We would start a campfire, have some beer, and fry up some squirrels or fish or whatever we caught that day. It was really a good time. It was a very simple time.

The work was very hard though. We had a garden which was an acre. There was a lot of work to maintain an acre garden. We also had a cornfield that was 2-1/2 acres, which I plowed every year with mules to plant the corn. We didn't have mules of our own, and I had to walk about 4 miles to a family friend's house to borrow their mules. I would go get their mules and bring them home for a few days, plow the garden and then the cornfield.   Then I would borrow them again when it was time to plow the weeds between the rows after everything came up.

When I was in the fifth grade, both my parents worked, so I would get home from school, and I would either plow in the garden or go up to the cornfield and plow corn. The cows also needed to be milked twice a day. I milked them first thing in the morning and again at night. Our family drank fresh milk, made homemade butter, and sold and delivered milk to a few people in town. We canned and processed everything we could from what we grew on our small farm.

My mom had a wood-burning cook stove only, so I was constantly splitting wood up into little pieces to burn as fuel.

Probably the worst thing in my life, though, was growing up with an alcoholic and abusive dad. He was not only mentally abusive but also physically abusive. I think those words are pretty much explanatory. He did work, but it was not enough to support the whole family. Our household always was in constant turmoil. We always lived in fear because we never knew when he was going to come home drunk and abusive. It was like walking on eggshells all the time.

Mom worked in shoe factories and such to support us, and we had a lot of struggles. Over time, I know she became a very angry person, having to work and provide for five kids and keep up the farm.

At times in the winter, my mom and I would be in the shed **LATE** into the nights. I would drag logs into the shed during the day, and my mom and I used a cross-cut saw to saw enough wood to keep the wood stove burning for heat as well as the wood stove used for cooking.

When I started school, I really struggled. In those days, I went to a two-room schoolhouse where first through fourth grades in one room and fifth to eighth in the other. I had trouble with spelling and writing. In the second grade, I was at a parent/teacher meeting with my mom. Right in front of me the teacher told my mom that I was very dumb and I probably would not amount to much more than a ditch digger. Those words really hurt me, and I began thinking, **"Why has God done this to me?!"** I was also left-handed, and they didn't believe anybody should be left-handed. That was back in the late 40s and early 50s. You have to realize, back then, teachers did not have to have a college degree. (I believe the teachers in Argyle were just high school graduates.)

They tried to force me to write with my right hand, and I couldn't. When I would write with my left hand, they would beat on my left hand with a ruler and, at times, make me sit at the back of the room for an hour with a dunce hat on my head. This was very humiliating and degrading for a young child as it takes away all of their self-worth and develops in them an attitude of worthlessness.

Home wasn't much better. I think my mom was struggling so bad trying to keep us all fed that she turned on me too. My angry mom and my alcoholic father constantly called me names and told me I was dumb, stupid and worthless. After a while, I too believed it. I became very angry at God, and I wondered to myself, "**How come I don't have the same chances as other kids? Why don't I have an opportunity to go to college?**" I gave up and quit trying to learn in the second grade. I thought, "**Why learn? I'll never have a good job; I'll never amount to anything.**"

That was pretty much how my whole childhood went. I worked very hard, not only doing my own chores. But I also worked on farms hauling hay, clearing off land with an ax, worked at a turkey farm, worked at a feed store, and I dug graves. As I got older, I worked at charcoal kilns loading cord wood into the kilns, which was very heavy work for a young man. The charcoal kiln was 8 miles from home, and since I didn't have a car, when my parents couldn't pick me up, I had to walk the 8 miles back home. I gave all of my wages to my mom to help her support the family. My parents were going to make me quit high school and work full-time in the charcoal kiln, but the day before I was to quit school, somebody turned me in for only being 16 years of age. It was illegal to do this type of work unless you were 18 or above. Can you imagine what this type of work would have done to my body at such a young age? I believe God was standing in the way of harm by having angels over me at this time.

Once you give up in life, you become angry. I became an angry child, but I kept most of my anger to myself. When I got to high school, it was not much different. They put me in a room with 20 other students who also had learning disabilities, some a lot worse than mine. The teachers didn't know there was such a thing as dyslexia, so they didn't care about educating us because they saw no hope for us; and when you were assigned to a room like that, the rest of the kids in school called it the dummy room, so the rest of the students made fun of us. One thing to my advantage was since I worked hard jobs most of my life, I was strong. I would fight if somebody tried to bully me, and I normally won. As a result, I really didn't have any trouble with being bullied.

High school was a very depressing time of my life. I had no hope, thinking I wasn't smart enough to go to college, and therefore, I would never have a good job. I knew I could never work in a factory. As a child, I built up a phobia of watching people go into a factory and that door shutting behind them. There is nothing wrong with working in a factory, but for some reason, I just couldn't. So I decided to join the military.

Grandpa John Brunnert's garage and car...one of the first cars in Argyle!

Jean and Joan at Argyle School

Twin

sisters

Jean

and Joan

Sister Jackie in Argyle

Jackie next to the washhouse

Our wash house and smoke house

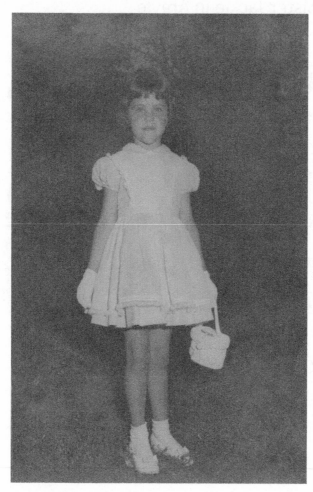

Sister Jackie in Argyle

Bob and sister Sharon in Argyle

Mom and Dad and twin sisters Jean and Joan

JOINING THE MARINE CORPS

On May 15th, 1960, I went to St. Louis and was inducted and sworn in. That night they put us on a plane. It was a prop plane. It took off in the daylight, and we were flying to San Diego, California, which was where I was going to go to boot camp. I fell asleep, and when I woke up, it was dark. I was startled by a red, glowing ring around the engine! I thought the engine was on fire! I didn't know that red glow was common to old prop planes.

I jumped up in my seat, and started looking around frantically to see if anyone else noticed. "Does anybody see that engine?" Everyone was pretty nonchalant, like nothing was going on, so I sat there and stared at the red ring for probably 10 or 15 minutes until I realized it wasn't a fire. That was the first time I had been on an airplane; the first time I had really been anywhere outside of Argyle. We landed in San Diego and were picked up in taxi cabs. It was about 2 o'clock in the morning, and I thought, "Wow! I've never been in a taxi cab either." This was a big uptown experience for me. We were taken to a restaurant and fed breakfast. I was thinking, "Man, I should have quit school and joined this outfit. This is really something." But that all changed pretty quickly. A Marine Corps vehicle pulled up; it was a big pickup truck with a cover over the truck bed and benches in the back. We all came out of the restaurant and were walking across the street. Guys were chewing gum and smoking cigarettes, and crap hit the fan right in the middle of the street. The Marine driving the truck started screaming at us, "Put those cigarettes out, spit out the gum, and get your ass in the back of that truck!" He was really ragging on us. It scared us to death, and I thought, "Boy, this guy is crazy. When we get to boot camp, I'm going to tell somebody about him." We got to boot camp and found there were six more just like him. We had a miserable night. We got all of our gear issued, our dungarees, our soap and everything we were going to need. We got a physical examination and had to bend over and cough. I think the Marine Corps uses that for a health check and IQ test. My attitude changed after coming out of the restaurant. They were running us all over the place and yelling, and I was thinking, "Man, I made a bad mistake here. I just want to go back home."

About 3 o'clock in the morning, they finally put us to bed. I was exhausted from the plane ride and fell asleep quickly. At 5 o'clock in the morning, the drill instructors turned the lights on and threw a metal trashcan down the aisles between the racks[1], and started yelling. I leaped out of that bed! They were telling us to get up, get our clothes on, get out the door, and get into a formation. I was scared to death. I looked at the guy right next to me, and he was sound asleep. I mean, he was **SOUND ASLEEP**. This drill instructor came down and looked at this guy, and I was thinking, "Oh, my God, they're going to kill him." I had my boots

---

[1] A rack is a framework for a bed, often stacked two high.

and clothes on and was buttoning my pants when the drill instructor just walked over, grabbed the rack, and turned it over. The guy rolled on the floor, and he was still asleep! I don't know what happened after that because I was running out the door to get in formation, and I thought they were going to kill him for sure. I never saw the guy again, so I guess he had some kind of sleep disorder, and they must have discharged him.

For the next couple of days, while we waited for them to get enough men together to form a platoon, we stayed in the barracks and scrubbed floors and cleaned all day long. Our supervisors harassed us as we scrubbed, waxed, polished brass, and did whatever needed done. While they yelled and hounded, we could see people through the window who were on the drill field, already in boot camp training. We thought, "Man, it's got to get better when we get out there."

Finally, they got enough people to form the platoon and we met our drill instructors. It was more of the same. They yelled, hollered, and kicked us in the butt if we weren't marching in step correctly. There was constant harassment all day long. We got up at 5 o'clock in the morning and had 5 or 10 minutes to shave, shower, dress, make the bed, grab our rifles, and be in formation. We learned to slip up under the sheet and not really disturb the bed to help speed up the morning routine.

Rifles were issued along with the rest of our equipment. After we got our rifles, every morning we would run, run, run around the grinder[2] with our rifles at port arms (rifles held out in front). The first morning we ran with our rifles at port arms, halfway around the grinder, recruits started dropping out. I was exhausted holding that rifle, and I started dropping back out of the formation, too. I heard a big commotion behind me, and there was a drill instructor

_____

[2] The "grinder" was a nickname for a half-mile square, massive parade ground.

who had a recruit by the nape of the neck and was kicking him in the butt! I got a sudden burst of energy, and the next thing I knew, I was up there with the leaders and got around that grinder in no time!

It was a long three months. It was rough, and it didn't get any better until we went out to the rifle range. Then, they began to ease up on us a little bit. We had probably five or six guys drop out of boot camp. It was very tough in those days, but the day we graduated, boy, we were proud. We had our khaki uniforms on, we were in a parade, and a lot of parents showed up. They read our names off now as Marines. The appreciation of that day and the feeling of pride was just tremendous. We didn't quit or give up, we pushed through all that harassment and pain, and now we had made it through boot camp. The struggle was worth it just to be called a Marine. It was really such a great accomplishment, especially since my father told me I would never be tough enough to make it.

ROBERT JAMES GANNON

Goodbye Argyle,
Hello Bootcamp Hell!

PFC ROBERT JAMES GANNON

PFC ROBERT JAMES GANNON

HAWAII TO THE PHILIPPINES

HAWAII

When I graduated from boot camp, I was sent to Camp Pendleton, California, where we had completed 30 days of infantry training, I had hoped the Marine Corps was going to send me to school, where I would get some training. I knew it was a remote possibility. Instead, I wound up in the Fourth Marines in the infantry, stationed in Hawaii, and received no schooling.

When I got there, I was assigned to Delta Company. As I entered the barracks, a guy said, "Wow, here he is. I'm getting rid of this BAR." He was referring to his Browning automatic rifle. It weighed about 20 pounds and carried 13 magazines. When loaded with 20 rounds of 30-caliber ammunition, they weighed about a pound each. I thought, "Here I go again. I always get the worst. It's just like God is constantly punishing me."

We went on some field training for a week or two. Carrying that BAR was tough. It was an extra 33 pounds in addition to the cumbersome pack on my back. I was in pretty good shape from boot camp, but there are some rugged mountains in Hawaii, and at times I was so exhausted from the extra weight that people had to help push me up some of those hills! That heavy weapon turned out to be a blessing when we went to the live firing range. I became extremely accurate in shooting it. The rifle range had pop-up targets attached to stakes. I was so good with the BAR that with only a few shots, I could not only hit the targets but also split the stakes holding up the targets! This was from a standing position, shooting from the hip.

When they decided to form a special squad of Marines to put on demonstrations for foreign dignitaries and congressmen visiting our Hawaiian base, I was selected to be part of the squad. Out of the 2000 Marines stationed there, only 13 of us were chosen. It was quite an honor. After thinking God was punishing me, I was now honored with this distinction.

We put on quite a few demonstrations to bleachers full of people. There were concrete bunkers (surrounded by coils of concentration wire) to represent the enemy, and gas-operated machine guns in those bunkers that just fired blanks. Jets flew overhead as predesignated explosives were ignited, just as if the jets were dropping bombs. Next, a team of Marines who had Bangalore torpedoes would blow a hole in the concentration wire. We would be laying down cover fire for them. This was live fire; it wasn't blanks.

The machine guns in the bunker would be firing away. Pop-up targets that were like real men who represented the enemy popped up to shoot back at us. Like I said, I got so good with that weapon that I started shooting the pop-up targets off of the stakes, and I put on a really good show. I had made PFC, and within a few months, I was promoted to lance corporal. I was on the demonstration team for over a year. As a lance corporal, I was promoted to a fire team leader. A Marine rifle squad consists of a squad leader and three fire teams of four men each. Even after I was made a fire team leader, I had to carry the BAR for a while because I was still on the special squad doing demonstrations.

I kept pressing forward, aggressively taking Marine Corps Institute (MCI) courses. These included courses on military tactics and strategies, as well as many other topics. I just kept taking the courses and passing them.

A new battalion was opened, and some of us were transferred to it. Because I was a lance corporal, and because of my experience, they made me a squad leader. It wasn't long before I was promoted to corporal. It normally took four to five years for someone to make corporal, and I made corporal in less than two years. I was doing well on my efficiency reports, so when my two years were up in Hawaii, I was transferred to the Philippines.

THE PHILIPPINES

In the Philippines, I worked as a guard in the ammo bunkers which were located out in the jungles. I didn't have to walk any posts because I was a corporal of the guard.

In rainy season, there were snakes all over the place. They killed one snake near the guard house that was 24 feet long and weighed 240 pounds. It was a python. We had cobras lying across the blacktop roads that led to the bunkers out in the jungle. They were trying to stay warm. These cobras weren't scared of anything. If we drove a Jeep right at them, they would just raise up in the road and strike at the Jeep.

There were monkeys, and they hated us. I remember the first day I was to take over as corporal of the guard. We had a Jeep, and on my shift, I would place Marines at five different posts located in the jungles. Every post had a telephone to call the guard house if there was trouble. After I got everyone posted on the first day, I was in the guard house filling out my log book. One of the Marines on post called in and said, "Corporal, you had better come out here. Monkeys are all around me."

Since it was my first day, I thought it was a prank. "Okay, I know this joke," I thought. "I'll be right there," I said, but as I hung the phone up, I laughed and thought, "Yeah, I'm not falling for this one."

It wasn't long before he called back and said, "Corporal, I'm going to leave this post if you don't get out here. These monkeys are now throwing stuff at me." I said, "Okay, I'll be right out there." And I thought, "Yeah, the monkeys are throwing stuff at you?" So, I didn't go. The third time he called and he was sounding desperate, and I thought, "I had better go out there." Sure enough, he was surrounded by monkeys in the trees, and they were throwing stuff like rocks and tree limbs at him. We had a pickup truck, I got him into it, and we went down the road a short distance until the monkeys left. The monkeys would come back around the guard house from time to time and do the same thing. For some reason, they just hated us. I don't know why. But man, they would be out there running at the guard house, howling and screaming at us. They would be in the trees throwing nuts, rocks, or whatever they could find at us.

It was really hot in the Philippines. When we were asleep, we had the doors to the guard house open to let a breeze flow through. One time, a large cobra slithered into the guard house. Luckily, somebody saw him and yelled, and everybody got on the top racks. We threw everything we could at the cobra. His head was about 2 feet off the ground, and his neck was spread. We threw boots, belts, shirts, pants, (anything we could get our hands on) at him. Finally, he headed out the door of the guard house. We shut the door and never left it open again, especially in rainy season.

There were two guard houses which were 4 miles apart. When I wasn't on duty during the day, I stayed in good shape by running down to the other guard house, visiting with the guys, and running back.

There was an Olympic-size pool right across from the barracks. On my days off, I also started swimming in the pool, up to 70-100 laps. I was asked to join the Marine swim team and I won the Interservice Championship swimming for the 400-meter.

I was also the training non-commissioned officer (NCO). Once a year, the Marines had to take a test on Marine tactics. As the Training NCO, I sorted, distributed, and graded the tests. I knew most of the answers and made a 98 on the test when I took it myself!

I BECOME A FATHER!

There was a beautiful Filipino girl I met named Catalina. We fell in love and married. I had my first child—a boy named Joe, who was born in the Philippines in 1964. Becoming a father for the first time of a robust baby boy who looked just like me was an indescribable event!

From there I was transferred to Camp Pendleton, California, where I joined Charlie Company First Recon.

SERGEANT ROBERT JAMES GANNON,
3rd from left, in the Philippines, 1964

BECOMING A RECON MARINE

I never intended or even thought about becoming a Reconnaissance (Recon) Marine, but I learned this well: the physical training was hell until we got into Recon shape. They still have the same saying today, "Becoming a Recon Marine guarantees two things: pain and misery." They were right!

Once I arrived at Camp Pendleton, they saw my test scores, and that I had won the 400-meter Interservice Championship. I believe this is why, when I checked in to get my orders, they were to Charlie Company, First Reconnaissance Battalion.

The instructors and staff of Charlie Company pride themselves in training entry-level Marines in the profession of arms in a safe, yet physically and academically challenging period of instruction. They believe that mastering the basics, accountability, and attention to detail are keys to providing the Fleet

Marine Force with the world's best-trained infantrymen.

I told them Recon was a volunteer unit and I wasn't going to volunteer. The instructors IMMEDIATELY took me in a back room to meet two officers. They wanted me to tell them why I didn't want to volunteer to join Recon. It didn't take them very long to convince me that I needed to volunteer.

I'll never forget my first day after joining Charlie Company, First Recon. I thought I was in pretty good shape. I had just come from the Philippines where I swam the 400-meter on the Marine team and ran 8 miles every other day, but I still wasn't prepared for that first day. I'll never forget it. We fell out for exercise that first morning and did one hour of hard-core calisthenics. This involved a set of high-intensity vigorous exercises followed by 20 pushups just as hard and fast as we could go in a repeating cycle that lasted an hour. At the time it was finally over, I was thinking, "My God, I made it!" I was **TIRED**!

But the nightmare was only to continue. I remember the sergeant in charge said, "Right face, double time, ho!" Away we went, 6 more miles up and down the mountains of California. The last couple of miles, I was so exhausted and began losing feeling in my lower body; I was just shuffling along. My arms were so tired, I couldn't even raise them up above my waist. I was physically totally exhausted and in pain. I would set little goals just to keep going. I would see a bush, a tree, or a rock, and I would say, "If I can just get to that rock, if I can just get to that bush; and somehow, I made it all the way. Thank God it was on Friday because Saturday morning I couldn't get out of bed. I was still totally exhausted. My arms, legs, and body were all aching and sore.

That was my first day in Recon. But after a couple of weeks, we got used to it, and we kind of started looking forward to the morning workouts. But I will say this: we ate all we wanted yet were all slimmed down to skin and bones.

The next three to four months were really tough. The training was physically brutal and mentally challenging. When we were not training, we were in a classroom learning.

Many Marines didn't make it through the training. We had to do a timed 1-mile swim with fins on. When we completed the swim, we physically had nothing left. We could not even stand for any period of time. We were beyond exhausted.

My main regret is that I didn't get to go to scuba and jump schools, even though I completed my pre-scuba training and was doing my pre-jump training. I received my orders for scuba school in Florida, and then on to Fort Benning, Georgia, for jump school. However, that all changed when my platoon, the third platoon, got orders to go to Vietnam.

When the day came to leave Camp Pendleton, we were in formation ready to board a ship for Vietnam when they called me to the office. They said since I was the only boy in my family, I didn't have go to Vietnam. If I wanted to go, I would have to sign a waiver. On the one hand, I was relieved at the news because I really didn't want to go; on the other hand, I didn't want someone else to have to go in my place. I also didn't want to live the rest of my life wondering if I had been a coward by choosing not to go. So, I signed the waiver and went to Vietnam. I am glad I did it. It would be hard, even still today, living with the thought that maybe I was a coward.

1942 USS GEORGE CLYMER APA-27 1967

WW II ★★★★★
KOREA ★★★★★★
VIETNAM ★★★

In Honor And Memory Of All Hands Who Bravely Served "The Lucky George"

USS GEORGE CLYMER VETERANS

When we got to Vietnam and began operating behind enemy lines, we developed what they now call hypersensitivity. It is caused by our minds staying on high alert. We would sleep and still be aware of everything going on around us. Any smell or snap of a branch would wake us. If a bird was singing and suddenly stopped, my mind would snap to attention. Guys would be sound asleep and need to cough. While still sleeping, they would roll their shirt up and stick it in their mouth to muffle the cough. We seldom spoke, we learned to speak with our hands.

For many of our missions, we spent days on top of a mountain monitoring the Viet Cong's activity in the valley below. Many times we would find temporary Viet Cong base camps, including shelters built for sleeping, set up on the mountain where we had planned to be for the next four days. All of our senses stayed constantly in high alert mode to survive. We never knew when the Viet Cong might show up.

On one of our missions, we were walking down a hard, packed trail when a single Viet Cong opened fire on us. We started to run down the trail when the lead Marine yelled, "Stop, hit the deck!" It was when he started to run, he had felt the ground soften and begin to give way, and he immediately realized something was wrong. The soft ground the Marine felt was a large hole, a pit-like grave, filled with sharpened bamboo stakes (called punji sticks) protruding up from the pit floor. One more step and he would have fallen into that pit, and his body would have been impaled by the sharp bamboo stakes. Because we operated under such extreme life-threatening conditions, we developed an almost innate sense of impending dangers. I am not sure if the Viet Cong who opened fire on us was killed when we fired back or if he just ran off.

We kind of started looking forward to the morning workouts. But I will say this: We ate all that we wanted yet were all slimmed down to skin and bones.

Sergeant Robert James Gannon
(top row, furthest right)

MY FIRST EXPERIENCES ON THE BATTLEFIELD

My first experience in war was in August of 1965. We boarded the USS Iwo Jima - Landing ship, Personnel, Helicopter (LPH), an amphibious assault ship in Hawaii, and headed for Vietnam. It was really a nice ship. Most troop transport ships have cramped spaces with hundreds of people in each compartment. Racks of beds can often reach five to eight rows high! Our ship had a nice compartment for our Recon platoon. There were just 18 of us. All of the beds were just two high. We had plenty of room. We were on the second deck down from the main deck, and the third deck was down from where the tank guys were located. There was a stairwell that lead from our deck down to their deck. I made really good friends with three of them in the week or two that we were on the Iwo Jima. We played cards together, we shot the bull together, we laughed together, and we became really good friends.

The first day of war was a battle called Operation Starlight, and it was a landing in Chu Lai, Vietnam. We weren't to go in on the first wave, but the tanker guys were. I visited with them that morning at breakfast. They were getting ready to leave for the battlefield, and I remember telling them something I regret saying today. I said, "Hey, guys, I'll bring a can opener with me in case that tank gets hit and you need somebody to cut you out." We all laughed and thought it was funny.

We were on the second deck when the battle started. Like I said, we weren't to go out yet. There was a ramp that would bring the casualties down from the main deck (the top of the ship) to the second deck where there was a large staging area. The ramp would go "beep, beep" and then lower down to the second deck. The second deck was where we were located, and our job was to help get the casualties off of the ramp. I remember the second time I heard the "beep, beep" sound, and the ramp came down, I saw three dead bodies. They were the bodies of my friends, the tanker guys. I just remember looking at them, and they were pale and whitish looking.

Incidents such as these change one's life forever. Before the battlefield, we didn't realize the seriousness of war. I was looking at them and thinking just an hour earlier we were joking and laughing together, and now they were dead. I would never forget. I was forever changed and will never be the same. My mind started building barriers and preventing me from getting too close or personally invested in others. Sadly, when we returned home, my mind was still in the same mode.

All of us began to build an emotional wall to dull our feelings for others and even our own family. I think to this day, those who served in war probably struggle to accept love and hugs and say the words, "I love you." I find it is even hard to purchase an emotional card—it's easier to give a humorous one. Seeing my friends dead on the ramps was the beginning of that protective wall for me, and it continued to build through my two tours in Vietnam. It has taken decades of my life to overcome that isolating instinct and ability to express feelings for others and my own family. I am now able to utter the words "I love you."

Shortly after witnessing the death of my three friends, we loaded onto helicopters and landed in the middle of a battlefield where over 600 Viet Cong soldiers lay dead. I kept thinking how many children will never again see their fathers. Mothers and wives will probably never know how their husbands and sons died. We passed through a village where the women and children had been caught in a crossfire between American and Viet Cong soldiers. No amount of training could ever prepare you for the horror of what happened to that village. The images of that horror would be forever imprinted in our minds. I felt like yelling out, **"God, if you are real; God, if you are real, why are you letting this happen?"**

We came to another village that had not been touched by the war. All the men were gone, maybe forced to fight with the Viet Cong? All the Vietnamese women were on their knees in a long line, holding up bits of food, crying and begging us for their lives. The Viet Cong had told them the Marines were called devil dogs and we would come into the village, rape them, and kill them all. I can't imagine what this day was like for these women with the battle being waged all around them and the horror of death surrounding their village. Many of their husbands and sons who had been forced to serve in the Viet Cong army had been killed. Now, foreign troops were entering their village. After misinformation was spread by the Viet Cong, the villagers were expecting us to kill them all—women, children and babies. I was standing in front of that line of the Vietnamese women trying to communicate to them that we were not going to harm anyone when one of the women tried to hand me her baby. She, too, was on her knees, holding her baby up and gently shaking it. She thought she could save her baby by giving it to me.

That's been over 50 years ago, and I still visualize this woman's face so clearly that if I were an artist, I could paint it even today. She made such a lasting impression on me as she was holding her baby. I can still see the panic in her eyes, the tears running all the way down her face to the ground, begging me in a language I could not understand. I knew what she was saying just as if she were speaking English as she offered me her child. She was saying, "Please take my baby, please take my baby, I want to save my baby's life." As I was looking at her and those tears running all the way down her face and dripping on the ground, I was thinking I had seen enough killing today, and I hope I never have to see any more. What was so impressive about her was she had no concern for her own life, just her baby's life.

A strange happening was when we turned to leave and had caused no harm, the women looked totally puzzled as we handed them some of our C-rations as we headed out of the village.

I again asked, "**God, where are you, where are you? If you're a loving god, why are you letting this happen?**"

Years later, in a deep depression, I asked God again, "**WHY, WHY, WHY** have you let such horrors happen on this earth?" The thought came to my mind that this is what happens when we allow evil to prevail.

"Take my baby, PLEASE TAKE MY BABY!"

FIRST DAY IN WAR, MISSION CONTINUED

We moved on and swept through another village. About halfway through the village, we found a Marine sitting on the ground. He had dropped his rifle and was crying. Right next to him was some kind of a cellar with a cover over it. We looked in it, and there was a dead Vietnamese woman and her baby, and her arms were still enveloping the baby. They both had been shot—the bullet passed through the baby's back and into the mother's chest. We couldn't get the Marine to talk. He was just sat there and crying uncontrollably. We tried to get him up, but he was so distraught he couldn't even get up.

Most of the people in the village had these cellar-type holes where they kept their supplies. The Viet Cong frequently used the cellars as hiding places. We don't know if he saw something move and shot in that direction or if he just opened the cellar and found the woman and her baby dead. We got him some medical help, and moved on. To this day I do not know what happened to him, but I think about him quite a bit, and I pray that he is okay. I knew the war was over for him—they were sure to send him home because of his mental condition. I knew, though, that the war of post-traumatic stress with its nightmares and flashbacks would rage on. I wonder to this day if he survived it or got through it with some kind of treatment. We thought it was possible he was in such a high state of anxiety, fear and self-preservation after fighting his way for 8 miles from the landing zone to the village where we found him, he probably experienced the Viet Cong popping out of the spider traps and holes, and when he opened the lid of the cellar and saw the movement, he just automatically shot.

We moved on and came to a big open field where we were going to spend the night. It was getting about dark when we were sitting in the field eating our C-rations, and the Viet Cong started dropping mortars on us. It was the first time I had ever been in mortar fire, and you could hear the **boom, boom, booms** as the mortars were fired, and then the SCREAMS of the shells started coming in. They started hitting the ground and exploding all around us, and the artillery fire just screamed as the shells fell. I remember lying on the ground panicking. A fear was rising from the bottom of my feet, and something in my mind kept screaming, "Don't let that fear get to your brain." It was like a ball of terror that started moving up my body to my knees and my waist, and I knew if it got to my brain I was going to break. The shells kept exploding all around us, and the dirt was flying—the concussion waves of the explosions felt like somebody was driving needles into our ears. I remember grabbing the tall grass and wrapping it around my hand, pulling myself flat to the ground so I couldn't get up. The fear worked its way all the way up to my throat. I was lying on the ground, pulling myself down so hard with that grass, I could feel it cutting into my hands; and my mind was screaming,

"Swallow! swallow! swallow! swallow!" I just kept swallowing as fast as I could, and finally it passed. The Viet Cong shelled us off and on for the rest of the night. I never experienced that again.

The next morning as we were moving out, I couldn't find my helmet. I walked past a big pile of the helmets, rifles, and clothing of men that had been killed or wounded. I saw a helmet, grabbed it and put it on my head. I knew immediately somebody had gotten killed in it because the smell of death was in that helmet. That smell of death lingered for the next three days.

Every time we came to a water hole, I scrubbed the helmet. I scrubbed it over and over again trying to get that smell of death out.

Our mission, when we left that field, was to go back through the battleground, as it was reported there were a lot of Viet Cong still hidden in spider traps. They had allowed the main force of Marines to pass by, and now they were creating havoc on the Marines who were trying to move supplies and equipment forward. The Viet Cong were popping up out of their spider traps[3] and shooting Marines.

It was our job to go back through, find them and eliminate them. We had to walk through that sea of decaying bodies. The stench was so bad for the next two days that I kept wondering **"Where is God? Is he really real?"** On our first day in war, we

---

[3] These spider traps were deep holes in the ground with a camouflage cover to look exactly as the ground around them. There was normally one Viet Cong to a hole, and he could pop up as the Marines passed by and shoot them in the back. Then the Viet Cong would drop back into the hole.

came off this nice, clean ship from a sort of idyllic backdrop that made our present surroundings seem impossible and unimaginable. We were all changed that day. For the rest of our lives; we would never be the same.

That was my first three days in war.

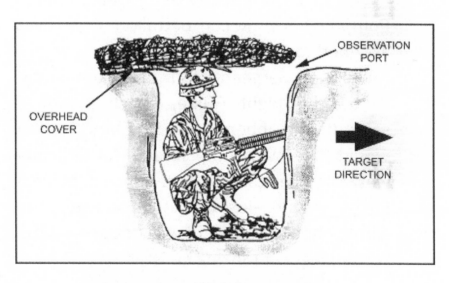

<u>Viet Cong Spider Trap</u>

THE MAN WHO CHANGED MY LIFE
(SERGEANT HOFF)

When I first joined Charlie Company, First Recon Battalion, I wasn't sure I could perform at such an elite level. Coming from a dysfunctional family and a background of dyslexia, I was not totally confident of my abilities.

I was a sergeant when I joined Charlie Company, First Recon Battalion, and I was assigned to the Third Platoon. This is where I met Staff Sergeant Hoff. I was appointed to be the Right Guide, which meant if something happened to Sergeant Hoff, I would take over the platoon. The difficulty was I had basically no experience in being a Recon Marine—less than anyone else in the whole platoon, but yet I was designated the second highest ranking enlisted man.

Sergeant Hoff was a battle-hardened Korean War veteran. We got along well and had a good time hanging out. We would have a few beers together after work and became great friends. I wasn't around the platoon much; I was attending Recon schools. Being a Recon Marine required more skills and training than I had ever expected: how to use radio communication, knowledge of topographical maps, understanding how to call air, ground artillery, and naval gunfire with the different effects of artillery shells and bombs. I could go on and on.

I was in training for three months. About 30 days of that was spent at Mountain Leadership School in Bridgeport, California. There we trained for cold weather combat, learning to fight in cold temperatures and in lots of snow. Much of our training was done while wearing snow shoes and skis. We also completed some mountaineer training where we learned about different types of rocks we might encounter in climbing and how to use pitons. One of the final tests we had to pass, was the ability to tie 22 different knots blindfolded.

I had been back on base for about a month after returning from Mountain Leadership School. During this time, I completed pre-scuba training and paratrooper training, and I was scheduled to leave in two weeks for scuba school in Florida. After that, I was to report to Fort Benning, Georgia, for paratrooper training. Instead, we received orders to go to Vietnam to join the 3rd battalion, 7th Marine regiment. On that day, Sergeant Hoff's attitude changed and he seemed to turn on me heavily. I suspect he was just trying to educate and prepare me in the event that I would need to replace him. Whenever I made a mistake or I didn't know the answer to one of his questions, he would yell harshly at me. All of the questions he asked were things needed for my team's survival.

For the next 30 days, I lived in hell as he pushed me to the level I needed to be in order to be able to survive. I thought this would get better when we arrived in Vietnam; but when we got to Vietnam, it only got worse. Every time we were assigned a mission, I drew up plans with him, and each mission behind enemy lines was very detailed. We planned for every possible deviation, and if I left out anything, he would hound me, "It's the little details that will save your team's life out there!"

We had been in Vietnam about three months when Sergeant Hoff was wounded. A bullet passed through one side of his body, nicked his spine, and came out the other side. He was sent to the U.S. Army Hospital in Japan. The next morning, they called me into the office and promoted me to platoon sergeant of the Third Platoon. I was shocked. I was only 24 years old. Most platoon sergeants are around 30 years old and a whole lot more experienced than I had. But I knew at that moment why Sergeant Hoff had pushed me so hard and my respect for him swelled.

One of the first missions I was to lead was extremely dangerous. A regiment of Viet Cong was suspected to be gathering in the valley to launch an attack. We were being sent in to confirm this and it was risky. A Viet Cong unit of this size would be patrolling their perimeters. Headquarters was sending us inside of those perimeters to gather the information they needed. We were dropped in on top of a hill and immediately started making our way down toward the valley.

We couldn't see through the jungle canopy, so I had one of my men climb a tree to peer down into the valley and determine if there was any activity going on. When he got about halfway up the tree, we heard a Viet Cong patrol talking. They were coming up the hill right towards us. I motioned for my man to come down. As he started down the tree, he stepped on a branch; it broke, and he began to fall. As he fell, he hit another branch right below it and let out a big groan, "**OHH!**" The Viet Cong stopped talking, and we knew they were now aware of our presence on top of the hill. They had probably received information a helicopter had dropped in a Recon team and were patrolling the area.

Sergeant Hoff had pushed me hard to make sure I planned to the smallest details and possible scenarios. Because of this, I was prepared. I had already preplanned all artillery concentrations according to our exact location. Had I not done this, precious time would have been lost calling in the coordinates. Because of this foresight, all I had to do was command artillery to fire at echo x-ray 272 or echo x-ray 271 (or whatever). Since the artillery already had the preplanned coordinates, they could start their fire immediately.

So when the Viet Cong were coming up the hill toward us. I called in the concentration number and told artillery to fire two volleys. The rounds fell short, and they were hitting and exploding all around us. Dirt was flying, trees were being hit; one artillery round hit a tree just to the left of me, about 20 or 30 feet off the ground, and the whole tree exploded. Bark and wood flew all over the place. The shells were hitting close around us, the concussion from the shells felt like needles going through our ears. We were all hugging the ground as tight as we could. It's beyond amazing that none of us were wounded.

After the second volley, we got up and started running. We knew Viet Cong were probably waiting to see if there was going to be a third volley before they got up, and this gave us a head start. I had already planned for an emergency landing zone. As we ran down the trail, we radioed to headquarters that we were heading for LZ1. They were to send helicopters to pick us up there.

The Viet Cong were closing in behind us, but I had also preplanned other artillery concentrations to be dropped on the trail. I had studied the topographical map in such detail I had memorized the terrain. As we ran past the first concentration point (I still remember that concentration number to this day!), I yelled to the radio man, "Tell them to fire echo x-ray 273!" Artillery shells started falling within minutes right behind us on the trail, thus blocking the Viet Cong and giving us more lead time. I had also preplanned two or three more concentrations.

Soon we got the information that two helicopters escorted by two jet fighters had been sent to pick us up. We beat them to the pickup point. We heard on the radio one of the helicopters was having trouble. When we could see the choppers approaching, we threw a smoke grenade which signaled where to pick us up.

The first chopper came in, and I loaded my men on it. As a sergeant, I made sure my men got on first, and I waited for the second chopper. When it arrived, I got on it with the rest of the team. The pilot was revving the engine, but the chopper wouldn't pick up; it just sat there. The pilot kept revving the engine again and again but nothing happened. The chopper would just move around a little bit. Everybody was getting nervous. We all sat on one side of the chopper, watching out the windows with our rifles, knowing the Viet Cong were going to be coming out of the jungle any minute and we were going to be a sitting target.

The crew chief of the helicopter screamed at the pilot, "**Get this thing off the ground! Get this thing off the ground!**" He couldn't get it off the ground. We were sitting on top of a hill, and he just started taxiing it down the hill. The chopper was flopping to the right, to the left; I don't know what kept it from turning over. It threw us out of our seats. We were all on the floor hanging on to the metal seat supports. He finally got the helicopter off the ground. The helicopter would lift a bit, and then it would start coming down. Again, the pilot would get it airborne, and then it would start coming down. I had my map in hand, trying to figure out where we were, because if this thing crashed, the Viet Cong were sure to be right on top of us.

Somehow, we made it all the way back to camp. We were about 10 feet off the ground when the helicopter fell with a "**BANG!**"

After that mission, I received a lot of accolades for my planning and the great job I did under duress. But I felt there was just one man deserving of the honor—Staff Sergeant Hoff. He had pushed me hard and I know now he truly believed in me. For the rest of my time in the Marine Corps, I was well respected for my leadership skills and superior knowledge of infantry tactics.

About 10 years after I was medically discharged from the Marine Corps, I made contact with Sergeant Hoff. He had retired from the Marines and was selling insurance in Oceanside, California. We were in the process of making plans to meet halfway between Missouri and California. About a week later, I woke up—I can't remember the date, but I will always remember the time: It was 2:30 in the morning. Something told me he had just died, and I never heard from him again. He was the person who gave me the courage to chase my dreams and go to college. I am forever grateful.

A RECONNAISSANCE (RECON)
PLATOON SERGEANT'S GOOD MEMORIES

Being a platoon sergeant in Recon was very different than being in the infantry. Recon personnel were exceptionally trained, had leadership skills, and in-depth knowledge of team operations. Most of the men knew my job well enough that if something happened to me, they could take over and continue the mission. Only one percent of enlisted Marines are selected to join Recon, and only one-half percent of them make it through the tough training. The result is a highly-skilled, ultra-disciplined team with determined, aggressive attitudes.[4] My job was mainly to receive the mission, to organize it, to plan the details from start to finish, and to make sure we had everything we needed. Being a platoon sergeant in Recon was made easier

---

[4] *It is official, the fittest unit in the Marine Corps is the 1st Reconnaissance Battalion, based in Camp Pendleton, California, winning the Corps' Superior Unit Physical Fitness Award.* Jan 27, 2020

because of the superior discipline and capabilities of the team.

The only trouble we had was when men train hard, they play hard; it seemed like every time we got liberty, we got in trouble. When we left California, our first stop was Okinawa. We were going to spend several days there, and everyone was secured to the base without liberty. We got a bunch of beer and were in the barracks about half-lit when the military police (MPs) came in with three of my men that had been caught in town. The guys had taken their trencher tool, dug a hole under the fence, and went to town on liberty. They were in pretty big trouble. The MPs brought them into the barracks. The MPs told me they caught them in town, they had their names, and they were going to write them up and take them to the battalion brig. I yelled at the men and asked them why they would disgrace the rest of us Recon Marines by digging under the fence. I became very aggressive, grabbing one of them and slamming him against a wall. I yelled in his face. I grabbed another one, banged him around and started yelling at him. I told the MPs, "Let me handle this." The MPs were in shock. They were looking at me like "Holy cow; man, this guy is crazy!" I said, "You guys can go ahead and leave. I'm going to take care of this, alright"? I think they were half scared of me, so they said, "Okay, sergeant, you take care of it. Looks like they are going to be in worse trouble with you than if they go before the battalion commander in the morning." They probably would have gotten busted or put in the brig if they went before the commander, so as soon as the shore patrol left the room, I smiled and said, "Alright guys, let's have more beer to celebrate my outstanding acting ability." We proceeded to drink most of the night.

We were in Vietnam for about three months when they pulled us out to participate in an amphibious landing. They loaded us onto a troop transport ship after living for three long months of risking our lives and living on the edge behind enemy lines in the jungles. All the men were wired—they were WIRED, they were WIRED! I mean, they would jump at anything.

They sent us to Hong Kong, and we were all in a bar. I can't remember exactly what happened or how the fight started, but Marine loyalties were strong—if one of us was in a fight, we were all in a fight. The police were called in. About 25 of us Marines and Sailors were loaded up in paddy cars and locked in cages. They took all of our money which happened to total the exact amount needed to pay for the damages we had incurred. Then, they hauled us back to the ship.

We were attached to H and S company (which is a headquarters and service company). There was a captain in charge of H and S company, and he already didn't like us. We were en route to the Philippines when he told us, "I'm not taking a chance on your men getting in any more trouble. When we get to the Philippines, you all are going to be on restriction."

When we got to the Philippines, there was a river separating the base from the town. They put us in a barracks right next to the river. Of course, we got a couple of cases of beer and started drinking. The next thing I knew, it seemed like men were disappearing. I looked out and saw a couple of duffle bags floating along the river. I don't know if they took all their clothes off or if they had on swimsuits, but the men were swimming across the river with their duffle bags toward town in search of booze and women! We had stocked up plenty of beer, and we drank for most of the night.

We had a young lieutenant whose name was Lieutenant Williams. I think he was a second lieutenant. He had graduated from West Point, and he was highly disciplined and regimented. There were 18 men in the Recon platoon. We had formation every morning and had to report if anybody was missing or absent. So, we were standing in formation, and out of 18 men I had 6. Here came Lieutenant Williams to get the morning report, and I began thinking, "What am I going to say? Nothing comes to mind." He just stood there with a puzzled look on his face. I saluted him and said, "We're all present and accounted for, sir." He saluted me back and said, "Sergeant Gannon, can I talk to you for a minute?" I said, "Yeah." And he said, "Where's everybody at?" I said, "Well, they went to town. They swam the river, but I'm sure they'll be back soon." He shook his head and said, "You know, Sergeant Gannon, this isn't the way I thought the Marine Corps was going to be."

I replied, "Sir, you have to realize these men are the elite of the elite.[5] They have gone through some of the toughest training in the world. They have a special personality. No matter how dangerous the mission, they never complain. We are under constant but silent fear of being captured

[5] See footnote #4 on page 79 in above document.

and tortured by the Viet Cong. You know, sir, when a team gets in trouble, every one of them will volunteer and be ready to go in and rescue, no matter the danger or the cost to their lives. They felt they were unjustly restricted by the H and S Company commander, and they were going to town at any cost. Since we were leaving here and going back to Vietnam, this could have been their last hurrah." He just looked at me and said, "Sergeant Gannon, I hope you're right about them returning."

It wasn't long before you could see the duffel bags coming back across the river, and by noon, they were all back except for Sergeant Hoff and our squad leader named Moffat. We were scheduled to board the ship the next day, but since a hurricane or typhoon was coming in, we were given orders to board the ship early. Sergeant Hoff and Corporal Moffat were still in town somewhere!

Before I was transferred to California to became a Recon Marine, my tour of duty had been in the Philippines. I had been on the Armed Forces Police and I still knew some of the guys. I used that advantage to speak to the Armed Forces police on behalf of Sergeant Hoff and Corporal Moffat. We went through all of the bars and couldn't find them until we searched the last one, right at the gate. There they were, sitting dead drunk.

I went in with the MPs and told Sergeant Hoff and Corporal Moffat, "Hey, you guys are under arrest. They sent me to town to find you, and we are taking you back to headquarters. They are probably going to put you in the brig." I was lying to them, of course, but they didn't know it. Boy, were they hot! They started calling me all kinds of names (which I can't mention because this is a Christian book)! We put them in back of the paddy wagon, shut the door, and locked them in. As we were going down the road toward the base, I could hear them back there yelling at me, calling me all kinds of names, and threatening my life. We finally got back and opened the door to let them out right in front of their own barracks. It wasn't until we reached the barracks that they realized it was a joke. So we had a few beers, and renewed our friendship.

The H and S Company commander still didn't like us. He was the one who put us on restriction and was always making snide remarks.

He and I had some confrontations. I noticed he was exercising with some of the Marines, and every morning he would be with a different group of Marines in H and S Company. I went to him and said, "Sir, why don't you come and exercise with us? I see that you are doing morning exercises with everybody else." For two or three mornings, he ignored me. I don't remember exactly what I said to him one morning, but I got kind of feisty and possibly insulted his manhood. The next morning, he showed up. He was coming at us with kind of a lively step and a grin on his face. I thanked him for coming, and as I looked at that grin on his face and at the shine in his eye, I was thinking, "Mister, you ain't gonna have no shine in your eye, there ain't gonna be no grin on your face, and there ain't gonna be no lively in your step an hour from now ."

Our exercise routine lasted between an hour and an hour and 15 minutes. It was continuous, hard and fast. After every set of calisthenics, we would do 20 hard and fast pushups, back up again and do something like jumping jacks, then back down for 20 hard pushups. I have to give him a little bit of credit for his resolve. At the third set (about 60 pushups), I noticed he was really, really struggling. About the fifth set when we went over 100 pushups, he could no longer even raise his body. He would just go down flat on the floor trying to push himself up, but his strength was gone. The more pain I could detect in his face, the more joy it brought to my heart, and I swear the Lord was telling me, "The hell with forgiveness and mercy, pour it on him!" I noticed the last set of jumping jacks we did, he couldn't even get his feet off the ground. I was looking, but I couldn't see any daylight under his feet. He was just barely moving, and his arms were flailing. When we were done, I walked over to him, and I thanked him for joining us. As he walked off, all he could do was shuffle, and you could see the pain in his face and the pain in his eyes. We didn't see him for a couple of days. We heard he was in sick bay, so boy, did we ever get even with him!

I think by pushing ourselves to our physical limits during those workouts, we developed both the leadership and discipline mentioned in 1 Corinthians 9:27: *"I discipline my body and keep it under control, lest after preaching to others, I myself should be disqualified."*

The whole platoon returned to our base in Chu Lai, Vietnam, and our camp was right on the sandy shore of the ocean. We got a request that they needed some Marines to haul equipment. They were going to build an officers' club, and they wanted some Marines from Recon. This was unheard of, but I knew the H and S company commander had a hand in this request. He was still trying to get even with us. I think we had about 10 men go to help load up. The supply trucks drove right by our base camp to where they were building the officers' club. I was out there once, and I noticed some of the Recon Marines were hiding in the bushes next to the road. As the first truck came by, cases of beer flew off the back of the truck into those bushes.

Another truck came by, and more cases of beer flew off the back of the truck at the same spot in the road. This seemed to be a repetitious pattern!

The next morning, we got the word that they were missing 25 cases of beer. When the Recon men got the beer, they went inside their tents, dug holes in the sand, and they buried all the beer under their bunks. The next morning, a crew showed up with a couple of officers, and they were mad as hell. They were looking for their 25 cases of beer, and they were going to search our tents. I took them through the tents, and they were looking in foot lockers, lockers, and everywhere, and I was thinking, "You're almost standing right on top of the beer." They spent an hour or two there, and they never did find the beer. I don't know what they did, but that was the last we ever heard from that captain. I think he gave up on us. A few weeks later, we got attached to the Third Recon in Da Nang, so we didn't have to worry about him anymore and all of his crap that he tried to pull on us.

That was Recon—tremendous men willing to train hard, fight in a heartbeat, and even give their lives. They were independent and hard headed. That determination also meant they were going to go to town and get liberty no matter the cost. Boy, did they party hard and get into plenty of trouble! These are some of the good memories I have of Recon.

A HEROIC HELICOPTER PILOT

This is the story of a heroic helicopter pilot that I witnessed. We were on a major operation. A couple of battalions of Marines were going to attack a large force of Viet Cong infantry. We were being dropped in behind enemy lines. As the Viet Cong would make their retreats, we would be in position to call artillery, naval gunfire, or our air to attack them. When the operation was over, we waited with an infantry company to be picked up by helicopter. We took our positions around a rice paddy for about two hours until the long-overdue helicopters arrived.

By this time, the Viet Cong had infiltrated two sides of our defenses. When the first chopper tried to land, the Viet Cong opened fire. The whole rice paddy was covered with tracer rounds from their surrounding enemy machine guns.

The tracer rounds were just streaking across rice paddy![6]

I heard on the radio that two Marines just to the right of our position were hit, seriously wounded and in desperate need of evacuation. I was thinking, "How in the hell is a helicopter going to land in all this Viet Cong gunfire?"

The first chopper came in and did try to land in the rice paddy, but it was hit before reaching the ground and had to pull out. I said to my radio man, "This is going to be bad for those two seriously wounded marines. No chopper will ever make it in here to pick them up with all this incoming fire across the rice paddy." No sooner than those words left my mouth, a second chopper came in across that rice paddy and landed right between machine guns and the two wounded Marines. The pilot was so close to our position, we could see his face. I watched him turn his head towards the

---

[6] Every fifth round loaded in a machine gun belt is a tracer round, and these are illuminated and can be seen.

machine gun fire, and those tracer rounds were coming directly at his chopper. We watched as they loaded the two Marines aboard. The chopper lifted off, and the Marines were taken back to the rear for medical attention. I was thinking, "That's one brave dude."

It was an impossible situation; I still can't fathom how that bullet-riddled chopper withstood such a bombardment. When the pilot turned and saw all the tracer rounds coming at him, he must have felt he was looking death in the face.

Some heroes get medals for bravery, but many don't. In war, a lot of people risk their lives performing extraordinary acts without recognition.

I hope that pilot was honored for his valor.

A POEM FROM A HELICOPTER PILOT'S WIFE

This poem was written by Janet Seahorn, whose husband was a helicopter pilot shot and wounded in the line of duty. Janet has her PhD in psychology and gives lectures on YouTube about posttraumatic stress disorder (PTSD).

SILENT SCREAMS

You cannot see a solid scream when looking from the outside; you might find a glimpse of it while peering deep into someone's eyes.

You cannot hear a solid scream in a noisy, crowded room.

But you may sense that if you sat down face-to-face, your heart may sense its painful tune.

You shall not feel a solid scream in this our fast-paced world, but if you wander near its anxious spirit, it may unfold.

We walk right past a suffering soul and often turn away—not strong enough to face the grief the world has made him or her pay.

For solid screams are not unique for those who fight to die, and a living warrior's hell to survive is left with those tears inside.

A BOB HOPE CHRISTMAS

In December of 1965, Bob Hope came to Chu Lai, Vietnam, where we were stationed in First Recon. Because the Viet Cong were all around the outskirts of that base, special precautions were taken to fly in. Most flew in on a C-130 with all of the seats removed. The seats were replaced with ropes that crossed the plane and passengers held onto the ropes while sitting on the floor of the aircraft. That was necessary, since the plane had to come in high above gunshot level and then plunge almost straight downward above the base. A metal grate runway was laid in the sand for landing. Taking off was the same way— the plane would bolt straight up in the air as passengers held onto the ropes, dangling straight down. It was a scary deal, but that's how it was done.

We had heard that Bob Hope had fallen off the stage in Da Nang and sprained his ankle. He wasn't expected to do any of his dance routines at Chu Lai because the ankle was badly swollen. I really admired Bob Hope coming to put on his show for us. I can't imagine most Hollywood movie stars coming in such conditions—sitting on the floor with their arms wrapped around ropes anticipating a scary descent. Plus, there was the danger of Viet Cong surrounding the base, constantly threatening incoming planes with the possibility of bullet spray. But they did it. They came.

We could see that Bob Hope had a huge wrap around his ankle, but as he put on the show, he did all the dance steps. He never missed a lick, and I can imagine that he was in a lot of pain. I have the highest respect for him. He was definitely a patriot and loved America and American troops.

DOC SCHRADER

Sometimes God's character is quietly obvious in someone. St Francis of Assisi put it this way—"Always preach the Gospel, use words when necessary."

I knew someone like that named Doc Schrader. He was our Recon Third Platoon Navy corpsman. He wasn't preachy, but every morning (when we weren't on patrol), we would see him sitting in front of his tent reading his Bible. He had a God-given kindness so real that it lit up his eyes and tumbled out in his speech. He never said anything bad about anyone. Godly love was evident as he went about his duties as a corpsman, taking care of the medical needs of the men of the third platoon.

Once on a Recon mission, his Recon team came across a Vietnamese woman who was having a difficult time giving birth. He knew the Recon team was in great danger of being detected in the area where they found the woman. He told the Recon team to move on and he would catch up later. He didn't want to endanger their lives, but he was not going to leave this woman. He was determined to help her deliver the baby. (The Recon team did stay with him until he delivered the baby.) Doc Schrader lived kindness, that was his way. The heart of Jesus was always shining in him.

I was transferred back to the states when my tour of duty was up, but Doc Schrader still had six months to go. I thought about him a lot through the years. About four years ago, I found out he was killed while on a Recon mission. A man who was on the last mission with him told me what happened. The morning of their patrol, Doc Schrader asked one of the men in the third platoon that was staying behind to meet him on the beach to talk. Doc Schrader told him that he wasn't coming back from this patrol. He handed the man a letter he had written and asked him to make sure it got to his family. The man tried to talk Doc Schrader out of going on the patrol. He offered to arrange a replacement with the company commander but Doc refused.

The patrol got into a firefight with the Viet Cong. One of the Viet Cong threw a grenade, and it landed just behind the Recon team. They didn't see the grenade land. There was an explosion, and when they turned and looked, they saw Doc Schrader had jumped on the grenade to save his team by giving his own life. Doc was an example of Christ-like love and sacrifice.

Doc Schrader's life had a positive effect on all who knew him. It's impossible to forget someone who never lost his temper, never said an unkind word, was always willing to give of himself, and never asked for anything in return. I asked myself for many years what made him so special? Why did he have such a positive effect on all who knew him? When his name is mentioned to those who served with him, their eyes and faces light up as they smile and tell the stories of how special he was.

Well, I think I now know the answer to why he was so special—he served God 24/7. God was first in all parts of his life, he did whatever God asked of him. Many days I have asked myself, "Why can't we all be like Doc Schrader?" What a great place this world would be to live in! But the answer is, it is very rare to see someone truly put God first in their life. I know in my case, I try to pray the rosary every day but many days, I make excuses to pray after I watch my favorite TV program, or when I'm less tired or busy. My friend Doc Schrader wasn't distracted from his time with God for any reason. God was first in all parts of his life, and that is why he was so special. That is why those who knew him will never forget him.

I don't know what the conversation was between him and God the night before he was killed, but we do know God asked him to give his life. The next day he carried out the mission without hesitancy. He gave his life so others could live.

John 15:13: "No one has greater love than this, to lay down his life for another.

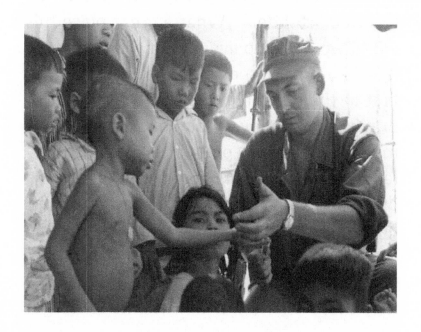

DOC SCHRADER

SERGEANT LEWIS

It was early 1966, during the rainy season in Vietnam. My Recon team was on a mission 37 miles from our base. On a normal mission, we would be out for five days and then be picked up by helicopter and returned to our base camp. It had been raining continually for a couple of weeks, as it was on this day also, and the cloud cover was so low, they could not get a helicopter in to pick us up. After eight days of waiting for the clouds to lift, we were notified the weather forecast looked the same for the next several days, and we were to start walking toward base camp. We knew we were going to lose radio contact once we dropped off the mountaintop onto the jungle floor. Military radios in those days had what they called line-of-sight contact and a range of only 10 miles. Being 37 miles from our base camp, we needed three radio relay teams spaced ten miles apart to relay any messages to headquarters.

Once we came off the mountain, we were told we would have no radio contact for about 27 miles of the 37 miles to base camp because they were also pulling in the radio relay teams to the base. The last 15 miles of our journey to base camp would be crossing open rice paddies. Trying to get through 15 miles of open country without being detected by the Viet Cong would not be easy. As we came off the mountain, we lost radio contact. I can tell you that is a very nerve racking and lonely situation being almost 37 miles from your base camp and in Viet Cong country without being able to call for help if we were spotted by the Viet Cong.

As it turned out, it was not the Viet Cong we had to worry about. We had two problems. Having been out on this mission for eight days, our supplies were running low, and when we got to the jungle floor, it was covered with leeches. They were not big leeches. They were anywhere from an inch to an inch and a half long. We had been in leeches before, so we knew what to do. We took our ammunition bandoliers, wrapped them around our legs, and sprayed mosquito repellent on our bandoliers. This would keep most of the leeches off our legs. The jungle floor was really hot, and we were sweating so much, the sweat and rain kept washing the mosquito repellent out of the bandoliers. We had to keep spraying the mosquito repellent every hour or so. By late afternoon, we ran out of mosquito repellent. It was not long before our lower body and legs were covered with leeches. When leeches fill up with blood, they can grow up to 10 times their body size. When they are full, they will drop off. They inject some chemical into the skin that causes the bites to continue weeping blood. It was not long before everyone's clothing from the waist down was covered in blood. We were slowly bleeding to death. Our corpsman kept reminding me if we didn't get out the jungle before nightfall we would bleed to death by morning.

The jungle canopy is so thick that at night it's like being in a cave. I couldn't see my hand an inch from my face. Unfortunately, we didn't make it out of the jungle before dark. I remember the corpsman telling me it's no use; since we can't see the trail, we should just stay together. He had me tell the men to make their peace with God since it was possible we would bleed to death in the night. I remember lying against a tree with the rain coming down just as it had done for the past eight days. I began thinking about my family and wondering if they would ever find out what had really happened to us, as all of our Recon missions were classified secret. I also remember thinking about all the good and bad I had done in my life. I sure had not done much to be proud of except serve my country. I began thinking if God gave me another chance, things would be different going forward. Our life is a story, and we are in charge of writing our own story. Experiences like this gave me the perspective to contemplate even today—

what would my story be if this was my last day on earth?

It continued to rain, and we were soaked to the bone. Normally, soaked as we were, I wouldn't have slept well. But instead of being shivering cold and awake all night, I fell into a deep sleep that lasted all night long. When we woke up in the morning, none of us had a leech on us, but we were weak from the loss of blood.

We got up and headed down the trail toward base camp. We only walked about a mile when we came out of the jungle to the open fields of rice paddies. I knew we were in real danger of being spotted by the Viet Cong while we tried crossing those 15 miles of open rice paddies. We were all extremely weak from the loss of blood, and if attacked, I was not sure how much of a fight we could put up.

We received a call on our radio. It was from Sergeant Lewis, the platoon sergeant of the first platoon. Sergeant Lewis and his Recon team had also been out for eight days, and they too had to walk back to base camp. He was only a few miles from base camp, when headquarters radioed Sergeant Lewis to ask if they had any radio contact with my team. He said no, but he and his team were going to head to the area of our mission and try to make contact with us. He was told not to do that by the command post and to keep heading back to base camp, that we had possibly been spotted by the Viet Cong and were probably all killed or captured. Sergeant Lewis refused to return to base camp, and he headed his team to where he thought we might be located. Sergeant Lewis's four-man Recon team walked all through the night, crossing about 15 miles of rice paddies, and made contact with us. It took us two days to cross the rice paddies to base camp because we were all so weak from the loss of blood. We hid out during the day and traveled at night. Twice we were attacked by small bands of Viet Cong, but we held them off. I am convinced we would not have made it back to base camp if it had not been for Sergeant

Lewis's help, as my Recon team probably would have been killed or captured. As it was, we were all so weak from blood loss, we were given the next seven days off to recuperate.

What's amazing about this story is Sergeant Lewis was a black sergeant. He grew up in the South in the 1940s and 1950s. The son of a sharecropper, they lived in a shack with a dirt floor. He lived in a time of segregated bathrooms, water fountains, and schools. There were not too many places blacks where allowed in. If they rode the bus, they had to sit in the back of the bus. The sick minds of the KKK could cause lots of trouble for them if they didn't walk the line.

Sergeant Lewis was a devoted Christian, and no amount of persecution could dim God's spirit in him. Because he was a devoted Christian and lived his life for Christ, and because of his faith and love for God, he didn't have the ability to hate another person. The same race of people who persecuted him, he risked his life to save. I wonder how many times, while crossing those 15 miles of rice paddies, he thought about what would happen to his wife and two daughters if he was killed. I have asked myself many times, if I had grown up under the same circumstances as Sergeant Lewis, would I have crossed those rice paddies? I am not sure. Sergeant Lewis had a special heart, the same heart as Jesus—willing to sacrifice his life so others may live. Sergeant Lewis was awarded the Silver Star, our nation's third highest award for his bravery.

THE CAPTURE OF THREE WOMEN

We were on a highly important mission that involved our entire platoon. This was the only time I recall our company commander ever being with us. We were at least 35 to 40 miles from our base and way beyond the range of artillery or naval gunfire.

There were to be three Recon teams patrolling, each with their own mission. My job, along with the radio man, was to set up my radio at the base camp so we could keep in contact with all three patrol teams, and if any team made contact with the Viet Cong, we could relay the message to the other two teams and all head out to a predetermined rendezvous point.

On the first day of the mission, all three teams had been gone less than an hour. They didn't make it very far from base camp when all three of the teams ran into Vietnamese women picking berries on the trail they were on, and they had to take them captive. One of the women was really a fighter and refused to walk. The team leader picked her up, threw her over his shoulder, and carried her back to our base. She was so scared that she peed as he was carrying her, and the backside of his clothes were soaked with urine. The company commander tried to abort the mission so we could get the hell out of the area because we figured that the villagers and the Viet Cong would come looking for these three women. We would be in trouble because we were beyond the range of any supportive artillery and naval gunfire. Since we were loaded down with a lot of communication equipment, we were to strictly avoid any type of combat being that far from any support. We were told to hold the women captive for the next three days while we were patrolling that area and gathering vital information that the headquarters company needed.

We all felt sorry for the women. They were scared to death and probably thinking they would be abused, and/or raped and then killed. One of the women had recently given birth, and she kept taking her breast out and squirting milk to let us know she had just had a baby she needed to take care of. We knew that other women in the village would be capable of caring for the baby. We had to tie them up with rope so they couldn't escape. Now the radio man and I not only had to worry about maintaining radio contact with all three Recon teams during the day, we also had three women to feed and take care of! We had to untie them at the times when they needed to use the bathroom which was at the edge of the camp.

By the second day, they calmed down. I guess they were starting to realize we were not going to harm them. They loved the way we cooked our food, and they seemed to love the C-rations we fed them. We used C-4, a plastic explosive, which could heat a can of our food in about 15 seconds. As soon as our matches touched the C-4, it would make a hissing noise and flare up a hot blue flame. The women would jump and laugh.

On the third day, our mission was up, and we were to head back to the landing zone to be picked up by helicopters and returned to base. We had a big decision to make. We were a 5- or 6-hour walk away from our pickup point. We knew if we released the women, they were only a short distance from the village, which was possibly heavily occupied by the Viet Cong. If the Viet Cong were in the village when the women returned and they had access to a military radio, we would be in a lot of trouble. The safest way to handle the situation would be to tie them up along the trail and hope for someone to find them. However, we had been there for three days and no one had come looking for them. We all agreed we didn't want to cause them any more stress than we had already put them through or chance that someone may not find them for the next day or two.

We untied them and pointed for them to go down the trail. We expected them to run like hell, but they walked a few steps, then turned back toward us and bowed with their hands together as in prayer to show us their thankfulness that we never did them any harm them. They did this five or six more times and then turned away and walked slowly down the trail. We were the ones that ran like hell because we knew if there were Viet Cong in the village, they would question them. If they had a radio, they would be sending patrols out looking for us.

These were the kind of men I served with in both tours of Vietnam. It saddens me the way Hollywood and movies have betrayed the Vietnam veteran and made him out to be a cold-blooded killer and a rapist. It is simply not true. The honorable men I served with treated these three women with the highest respect; none of them were touched, none of them were abused. We fed them, we took care of them, and we risked our lives by letting them leave freely to avoid more undue stress. This is a memory I have of the men I served with—kind, gentle and tough as nails!

THE BRUTALITY OF THE VIET CONG

As Recon Marines, it meant all of our missions were behind enemy lines. Many times we had to witness the brutality of the communist Viet Cong. They maintained control by fear, they had no rules other than to maintain control. The Viet Cong were a guerilla force also supported by regular North Vietnamese army. They raided the villages they encountered, stealing their rice and forcing the men to join the North Vietnamese guerrillas, gaining control through violence, threats, and fear.

One of the brutal tortures of the Vietnamese people we witnessed was while we were monitoring the amount of enemy activity at a village of rice farmers. We watched as the Viet Cong drove posts into the rice paddies. They then tied the farmers' arms together, stretched them high above their heads, and tied their arms to the top of the post. They were left hanging there for over 12 hours before they were cut loose. The farmers just fell to the ground and appeared to be unconscious to say the least.

On another of our missions, we were to watch for enemy activity at a village about 15 miles from our lines. On the second day of our mission, about 15 Viet Cong came out of the jungle and began to train in the rice paddy in front of the village. We called in artillery and several of the Viet Cong were killed.

We continued to observe the village and later that night, we heard shots and screams coming from the village. We knew the villagers were being tortured and killed by the Viet Cong because they thought someone in the village had used a radio to call in the artillery barrage that killed some of their soldiers. I can't explain the depth of despair, knowing we were the cause of the villagers being tortured and killed. Those feelings still haunt me today.

I remember praying to God to please intervene and stop the madness. The attack on the villagers went on for hours. There were only four of us on this mission, but every man was willing to try to stop the torture and killing of the innocent villagers, even though there would not have been much chance of our survival. It was a tough decision I had to make. I knew if we intervened we would probably all be killed and it would likely have caused a lot more problems for the villagers and made what we heard and saw seem minor in comparison.

Even though it's been over 50 years now since the torture and killing of the villagers, in my mind I still spend a lot of days on that hill overlooking the village, listening to their screams and cries and wondering if I made the right decision. My only comfort is that my men were spared from dying in a foreign land, for a foreign people. I think we still all live with some anguish and guilt over not being able to stop the torture and killing of the innocent villagers.

THE SNIPER

As Recon Marines operating behind enemy lines, we always tried to stay out of open country to avoid detection and being attacked. In those days, we operated in only four-man teams, and if detected, we did not stand much of a chance of survival.

On one of our missions, we had to cross through an open area and a couple of small rice paddies where we knew there was a high concentration of Viet Cong soldiers in the area. We were going to cross one man at a time, running as fast as we could down a 2-foot path between two rice paddies.

When it was my turn to cross, and I was running full speed. I was about three quarters of the way across the paddy when I stumbled, with my body leaning to the right. As I stumbled, I heard a shot from a Viet Cong sniper that was cutting down on me. Bullets make a whirring noise, and I heard the bullet pass where my head would have been if I had not stumbled.

Once I got across the rice paddy, I remember gratefully thinking: "God must have a plan for me."

THE SUICIDE MISSION

We were three days into our prior mission when we got a message over the radio telling us it was cancelled. We were being redirected to a new mission—to assassinate a North Vietnamese general who would be traveling with several hundred Viet Cong soldiers. We received the coordinates of the route which he would be traveling, and headquarters gave us a description of their formation.

There would be two small groups: the first would have 2 to 5 men, and the second would be a larger formation with 10 to 15 men. A third group would be a large formation of about 200 Viet Cong soldiers, and the general would be with that group. They gave a lot of identifying details about him, but most notably, he had a unique uniform with red shoulder pads.

This was a suicide mission. They were going to sacrifice a Recon team in exchange for this general's life. Once we fired and killed the general, we would be attacked by 200 Viet Cong soldiers. There were only 6 of us. Since we were 40 miles from any base camp, there would be no calling for help, no type of artillery support. We were never designed to be a fighting force. Our mission was to gather information, so the large part of what we carried was radio equipment along with our food and water. We only had 240 rounds of ammunition per man and 3 hand grenades; 240 rounds might sound like a lot, but it would be gone in a matter of about 20 minutes. If spotted, the Viet Cong would surely launch a frontal assault on us, so our chance of survival would be nonexistent. As I explained the mission to the men, I could see the look on their faces when they, too, realized this was a suicide mission. But no one complained. We knew we would be sacrificing our lives but saving the lives of other soldiers.

We walked for the rest of the day to get in our ambush position. We reached the position at dusk. It was a wet, muddy swamp. It didn't take long before we were soaked from the waist down and covered in mud. We tried to sleep sitting up, lying against some trees that grew in the swamp, so at least our upper bodies would be dry. As it got dark, we were attacked by hordes of mosquitoes. They were so thick, they covered our faces and got into our noses. We would wipe our hands across our faces, and they would be covered with dead mosquitoes and blood. We had mosquito repellent, but it didn't deter these mosquitoes. There were so many the repellent didn't matter, or the mosquitoes actually liked it!

As the sun rose in the morning, I looked down the line of men, and their faces were all swollen like mine from mosquito bites. One Marine's eyes were nearly swollen shut. We didn't have to wait very long before two Viet Cong soldiers passed our position, and every man slid his rifle to his shoulder. I remember looking at the sun rising in the sky and saying, "Take a good look, take a good look, because this is going to be the last sunrise we are ever going to see." I prayed this prayer: "God, I'm not asking you to spare my life; I'm asking you to give me the courage that I will need today. Please Lord, don't let my courage fail me. Let me go down fighting as bravely as the other Marines have fought before me."

Then I prayed for God to look after my children and ease the pain of their loss. I asked God to bring someone into their lives who would love them as I did; someone who would help them chase their dreams, push them to get good grades, and just give them a good chance in life. Again, all of our missions were classified secret, so our families would never know how we died.

In the end, we were blessed. The general must have changed his route before reaching the ambush spot. We waited more than 6 hours, but he never passed by. What an honor was bestowed on me to serve with men who were willing to die for their country to save the lives of others without complaining.

These men were only 19 to 21 years old but they had a sense of duty, courage, and a compassionate heart. They loved their country, and they were willing to die for it.

THE VILLAGE OF NIGHTMARES

It was in the early months of 1966. A large number of Viet Cong had been reported about 10 to 12 miles from our base, and it was thought they might be planning an attack on the base. So I was sent to that region with three other Recon Marines to try to locate the Viet Cong. We were dropped in by helicopter and made our way to a small mountain overlooking a large rice paddy, and on the south side of the rice paddy was a village.

The second day of our mission, about 40 Viet Cong came out of the jungle and began training in the rice paddy directly below us. I made a decision to call artillery on the Viet Cong. I had sixteen 155 mm howitzers assigned to this mission. Most of the time you call for one spot around because the accuracy of artillery rounds can be affected by wind, humidity, and other factors. Normally you fire a spot around and then make needed corrections. But I knew if I fired the spot around, the Viet Cong would just head for the jungles before we could inflict any damage on them, so I made the decision to fire all 16 guns. The rounds fell a little short of the target landing mostly in the village; and before we could command the artillery to "cease fire," they fired a second volley. I remember praying, **"PLEASE, PLEASE GOD, don't let these rounds hit the village."** There was a short silence, and another 16 rounds hit the village. The artillery rounds pretty much destroyed the village. We watched in horror as houses were blown up and fires were started. The rest of the day and throughout the night, we heard the screams and cries of women and children who were badly hurt, traumatized, and/or dying. Sometime during that night, I heard the long, almost nonhuman, wail of a woman—that wail has haunted me in my daytime flashbacks and nightmares 50+ years.

The next day we watched a long procession carrying the bodies of the dead to the cemetery. These were just innocent farmers who wanted no part of this war.

They just wanted to raise their rice and their families, and now many were killed or wounded, and many of their homes were destroyed. I was in a state of shock over the devastation that had taken place. I was 24 years old at the time, and I had just killed a lot of innocent people including women and children.

I never told anyone what happened to the village. I kept it a secret, even from my family and my closest friends. For the next 50 years, I was haunted with nightmares and daytime flashbacks of what had happened, and the wail of that woman. This tormented me so much that I thought of committing suicide.

I was medically discharged because of an injury during my second tour in Vietnam. Soon after leaving the Marines, my nightmares began, and mysteriously, at times, a little girl would appear in my dreams. I noticed there was a scar on the left side of her face. I did not recognize her as any child I had ever known. She would just stand there and stare at me with no expression or emotion. I always thought she was from the village, and I would try to reach out to hold her and tell her I was sorry; but each time I reached out to hold her, she would disappear. I was always confused because she didn't look Vietnamese but rather looked like an American child.

In addition to nightmares, I was having daytime flashbacks of that terrible incident in the village. The distressed sounds of the Vietnamese people played over and over in my mind like a recording for weeks at a time. This would send me into a deep depression. I still couldn't tell anyone what had happened, not even my family and children. The isolation and pain of it all caused me to distance myself from them. I seldom went to any family functions. Many times I would tell them I was coming, but I just couldn't go. I even stopped visiting my children. My posttraumatic stress was intense.

At one point, while working for the pipeline, I was staying in a motel located just 2 miles from my son's home, yet I still couldn't bring myself to visit him. I didn't understand why this emotional barrier existed, but I began to realize the seriousness of my posttraumatic stress disorder.

I only slept about 3 hours a night. I would go to bed at midnight and wake up about 3 o'clock in the morning. I was always the first one to work. The defenses I had intact were just as real as those on the battlefield, and I had no close relationships with anyone. I also had a severe case of hypersensitivity from those years in the jungles as a Recon Marine develops this as a necessity to stay alive. Any sound, day or night, would send me perceived fear of possible danger. At times, in severe cases, hypersensitivity would cause me extreme anxiety resulting in actions such as hitting the ground or ducking. Like many veterans with posttraumatic stress disorder, my coping mechanism was alcohol for many years.

Holidays were always bad. I would think of the men I had lost in Vietnam and the insurmountable sorrows their families must endure on these special holidays. The village would always haunt me at Christmastime—the families affected, the extent of their injuries, the children killed, severely wounded, or traumatized. I didn't feel I had the right to celebrate Christmas. I didn't want to buy anybody anything; I didn't want to receive anything—I just wanted to be alone.

AMPHIBIOUS LANDING

We had boarded the USS Iwo Jima, a helicopter carrier, in Okinawa , and we headed to South Vietnam. The day we pulled into the harbor where we were going to make the landing, the jets were already strafing[7] the beaches and the jungles behind them. As we were watching the jets strafe the beaches, just an eerie silence hovered over the whole ship as we all were watching and wondering what tomorrow would bring. We were all hoping those jets would wipe all the Viet Cong out so none of us would have to die tomorrow.

That night in our troop compartments, everybody was really quiet. Marines were writing their last letters home. Chaplains from all walks of faith were coming through the troop compartments talking to people, and all the conversation was really low. There was no laughter, no jokes; there was no real joy. There was only that eerie

---

[7] Strafing is a military term which means to attack repeatedly with bombs or machine gun fire from low-flying aircraft.

silence again like other times before a battle with the men thinking about their lives and family. Everybody had that same serious look on their face. When people did talk, they all spoke in low tones so as not to disturb anybody.

None of us slept much that night. We were hoping the night would pass slowly or never end, but it seemed like the night just sped by, and it wasn't long until it was morning. They got us up, we got dressed, and they fed us steak and eggs, which is unusual, so that kind of spooked us. We got

---

[8] *Absolution is when you are forgiven of all your sins and you are free. (Catholic Encyclopedia)*

[9] This phase is sometimes a very dangerous one in amphibious operations both for the crew of the boat and the men coming down the nets, especially when there are high seas. The boats bob about like corks and crash against the APA (Personnel Attack Ship). At one moment the net will be hanging clear of the bottom of the boat and at the next the boat will be raised by a wave so that the net is bunched up and the soldier with all his equipment may get a considerable shoving around.

our gear, rifles and all of our equipment together and headed up on the deck. When we arrived there were quite a few chaplains including Baptist, Pentecostal, and so forth, as well as a Catholic priest. As Catholics, we all gathered on one side, and the priest gave a short, upbeat talk to us and gave us all absolution.[8] I was in the first group of men as we went over the side of the ship on the nets and climbed down the nets into the boats.[9] When you are one of the first and your boat is full, your boat leaves the ship and goes off and circles and circles until the rest of the troops have climbed down the nets into the remaining boats. I remember thinking as we were circling, "I hope we circle forever."

Everyone is wondering how bad it is going to be when you hit the beach—are you going to be met with machine guns waiting for you as soon as the ramp is dropped, or are we even going to make it off of the boat without being killed? When everyone is unloaded from the ship and into the boats that are going to make the landing in, we broke the circles and headed for the beach. For sure, chills ran through our bodies when they gave the command "lock and load" which means to put a round in your gun's chamber. As I looked down through the boat, I could tell who was Catholic because we all had our finger rosaries on our dog tag chains. I think everybody was praying because of the unknown fear of just facing their first amphibious landing. Of all the helicopter landings I have been in, nothing compared to the anxiety and the fear of an amphibious landing. We were all praying for the strength and courage to do our job. You had this feeling come over you like there was nobody who could help you anymore, NOBODY. The only person who could help you now was GOD. We landed on the beach and faced light resistance. While we were still on the beachhead, the Viet Cong started dropping mortars on us. A mortar round hit between me and a Marine alongside of me, and he lost it. He just fell apart. I didn't know who he was, and I guess he had all he could take. He threw his rifle down and started running and just screaming, running down the beach. He totally broke. I was really mad at him, you know, I was angry. I thought, "We ought to throw him in the brig for the rest of his life," but today I realize that could happen to any of us, that any of us could get in that situation where you've probably just had enough and fear totally overtakes you.

We were lucky that day. The jet strafing of the beach had done a good job, we faced light resistance, and we were able to move off the beach and inland without too many casualties. I know this was nothing like the World War II veterans had gone through. They had beach landings where thousands were killed before they even made it to the beach. Our landing was nothing compared to their landings. I don't think we lost but a very few men during the whole landing, but I am just amazed at the bravery that the World War II veterans had at landing on Iwo Jima with 4000 casualties, Tarawa and the rest of them—what it was like to go in and thousands and thousands of Japanese were waiting for you with machine guns and artillery fire. Their first waves of boats generally never even made it to the beach. Thousands were killed. You hear the stories of soldiers climbing over the bodies of their dead comrades as they moved inland. The courage they had was unmeasurable. I heard that Chester Nimitz, a World War II Navy Fleet Admiral who served in the battle of Iwo Jima, said that uncommon valor was a common virtue on that day. It makes you think of the high cost of freedom that has been paid, and it kind of makes you angry when people in this country don't even understand and/or are not more grateful for the price that was paid for our freedom.

This phase is sometimes a very dangerous one in amphibious operations both for the crew of the boat and the men coming down the nets, especially when there are high seas. (Also refer to footnote 9 above in this document.)

This was my Marine Sergeant's Prayer:

God, I ask you not for any special grace on this day. But, if I should fall, I ask you to look after and protect my family, see to it that my children know love, and give them the discipline, education, and courage they need to fulfill their destiny on this earth. Please Lord, give me the courage and knowledge that I need to lead my men on this day so that we bring honor to our country, families, and the Marine Corps. I also ask you that if my courage should fail me, don't let me leave this battlefield alive, for I would like my men to remember me as a proud sergeant with the same courage and pride that I tried to instill in them. For Lord, if my courage did fail me and I lived, the shame would be too great. I could never face my family, friends, or my men again. I would just be a shell of a man just waiting to die. If some of my men do die on this day, have special mercy on them, for they have already spent their time in this hell called war. I would like to thank you for letting me be born in a free nation and all the good times that I have had with my family and friends. I also want to thank you for allowing me the honor to serve you and my country. AMEN

(I wrote this prayer the night before we made the amphibious landing. I then folded it and put it in my sea bag as to document to my children the feelings and responsibilities I had as a platoon sergeant before leading my men into battle. As my children were very young and didn't know me, I left this prayer for them to be proud of me because this would be the only true image of my sense of duty for the welfare of my comrades and the deep love of my children they would know.)

THE ELEPHANT GRASS

I had an experience that somewhat helped me relate to what Jesus went through in the Garden of Gethsemane. This helped me understand what a great love that God has for us.

Our Recon team had been on a mission for five days. We were about 20 miles from our base camp. It was late in the day when a helicopter was to pick us up. The chopper arrived about dark, but as he was landing, something malfunctioned and the chopper crashed. We were informed by the command post to destroy the chopper's communication equipment and find a good hiding place because it would be the next morning before they could get another chopper in to pick us up.

We knew the Viet Cong saw the chopper crash, and they would be looking for us. As I previously said, we knew they wanted to capture a Recon team because of all the damage we had caused in their supply lines; they had to resort to moving their supplies at night. We also located some of their training camps and had them bombed. We would listen to their propaganda on our radio back in base camp to a program called "Hanoi Hannah." It was broadcast in English. At times she would mention they saw a chopper drop a Recon team in, and she would let us know they were looking for us. The fear of being captured was always on our minds because we knew we would be severely tortured because of the hatred they had for us.

By the time we got the chopper's communication equipment destroyed, the Viet Cong began firing on us from the mountain next to where the chopper had crashed. As dark settled in, I moved the men into a field where about 20 acres of elephant grass existed. I told them to not move or start shooting unless we were stepped on by the Viet Cong.

The elephant grass gets about 10 to 12 feet tall and is real thick, so it is very difficult to move through because of its height and thickness. About an hour after we got settled in, we could hear the Viet Cong talking, and then we smelled smoke. We knew the Viet Cong were trying to set the elephant grass on fire to burn us out. But the elephant grass was too green to burn, so they began using machetes to cut through the elephant grass as they searched for us. Twice that night, the Viet Cong passed within a few yards of us. I remember my heart beating so hard, I thought surely they could hear it beating.

I remember wondering who I would be if I got captured; I was the platoon sergeant. The men would be looking up to me to set the example, and I kept thinking, "Would I be able to stand up to the torture? Would I be the brave, tough Recon platoon sergeant I was supposed to be, or would I just be a sobbing coward?" I began praying that if the Viet Cong did find us, let me be killed in the fire fight; I don't want to take this test and am not sure who I would be.

As I read about Jesus in agony in the Garden of Gethsemane, I remember how afraid I was that night in the elephant grass. Because of that, I can relate to some of the stress that Jesus suffered in dread of the crucifixion. Matthew 26:39—*He threw himself on the ground and prayed, "My father, if possible, let this cup pass from me; yet not what I want but what you want."* Three times in the garden he prayed that this cup be taken from him. At Luke 22:43, we read an angel was sent from heaven to strengthen him. In Luke 22:24, we read that in agony he prayed so earnestly, his sweat was as great drops of blood falling to the ground. I don't think we realize how much sorrow, grief, and pain he foresaw before he was taken captive. You see, Jesus was as human as me with the same fears and doubts I believe as I had that night in the elephant grass. The only difference was, he had all of our salvation depending on him being able to withstand the brutal torture of the crucifixion.

Saint Faustina, who Jesus took to the crucifixion, describes one scene where Jesus was standing before her, stripped of his clothes, his body was completely covered with wounds, and you could see bones on his back where the whips had torn the flesh off his body. His eyes were flooded with tears and blood. His face was disfigured and covered with spit. Still, Jesus chose to go through the crucifixion knowing we would be a rebellious and sinful people. His love for us is so great it is beyond our understanding.

As for the end of this story about the indescribable fear we had in the elephant grass that night, by some miracle, the Viet Cong didn't find us and gave up looking. The next morning we were able to crawl out of the elephant grass and escape!

DEFINING COMRADERY THROUGH THE SPIRIT OF GOD

The Bible tells us we are made in the image of God. It is during times of greatest difficulty we are being shaped into the person He means for us to be. During the challenges of war, that spirit of God shone through the men and women serving alongside me; they were willing to share what they had, willing to give their life to save another, courageously sacrificing all for the freedom of others. We call that spirit comradery—His divine nature in us. What a great place this world would be if that spirit would shine through us all 24/7.

I will never forget the day my first tour was up in Vietnam. I was a Recon Marine with over 35 missions behind enemy lines. I said my good-byes and was in a Jeep headed for the airport for my flight back home to the states. As I sat in the Jeep, I broke down and started crying. I didn't want to leave, even though the stress of a Recon Marine was unreal. Our normal routine was four days behind enemy lines, five days back preparing for our next mission, and then five days out again. On each mission, we knew the Viet Cong probably saw the helicopter drop us in, and they would be looking for us. The chopper would make two or three dummy drop landings so they would not know at which landing we were dropped off. The first day we were dropped in, we ran fast and hard as possible to get a distance away from the drop-off point with our senses fully engaged to detect anything amiss.

We knew the Viet Cong were hoping to capture a Recon team because of all the damage we had caused on their supply lines. They could no longer move supplies during the day. Our main fear was not death; it was being captured and tortured. Even through all of that, I still didn't want to leave. I had witnessed the spirit of God in each one of my fellow soldiers. Through the hardships and danger that we faced, love and closeness grew. Any one of them would have given their own life to save another. We shared everything.

RECON MARINES' VOW

Before each mission we vowed: "We're all going in together, we're all coming back together, or we're all going to die together, and we will never leave a brother behind."

That kind of closeness and loyalty is a once-in-a-lifetime experience. That made reentry into the civilian life challenging, and relationships were lacking. It was a totally different world. The kind of love and compassion we had experienced was mostly missing from society. It's been more than 50 years since I left Vietnam, and I still miss the men I served with.

COMING HOME AFTER FIRST TOUR

CAMP LEJEUNE, NORTH CAROLINA
JOB: BUTT NCO[10]

After my first tour was up with Charlie Company, First Recon, I was transferred to Camp Lejeune, North Carolina. I had a great job there. I was assigned to the rifle range, and my job title was Butt NCO. Each company had to retrain once a year on marksmanship training.

The job was easy, and I really enjoyed it. There was a lot of good fishing right behind the rifle range. There was a big bay, and when the tide was going out, we could go back there and just catch a cooler full of red snapper. I bought a surf rod because there was a lot of surf fishing along the coast. It was a great place, and when you transfer back from Vietnam, they give you a list of a couple of duty stations that you

---

[10] "Butt" NCO (or CBO for Chief Butts Officer) is responsible for the control and running of the target gallery and has a duty of care relating to all personnel under instruction. The butts area is the target gallery area.

would like to go to, so I had put down inspector/instructor duty which would be to train reservists.

JOB 1: INSPECTOR/INSTRUCTOR, TRAINING RESERVES

JOB 2: TOYS FOR TOTS, WORKING WITH MRS. DUPONT

I was on the rifle range for about six months, then I got my orders to go to inspector/instructor duty in Wilmington, Delaware, to a reserve training center. At that reserve training center we had many duties besides training reserves. We were the color guard for the parades and football games, just a lot of stuff like that. I was also in charge of the Toys for Tots program which basically was just me, and after Christmas was over, Sears and Penney's and stores like that would give toys to the Marine Corps. We were working really closely with the Dupont family, especially Mrs. Dupont, and they would rent big storage lockers. I would take this big 6 x 6

Marine truck and go down to Sears and pick up all the toys that were left over from Christmas, load them in a truck, take them down to the big storage lockers they had, and go to Penney's and do the same thing.

I got to meet Mrs. Dupont several times because the Duponts also donated a lot of toys and money for the Toys for Tots program. She was a really, really a nice lady. She lived in a huge house; it was beautiful. I guess you could call it a mansion. But she was really humble. I had to go over there to meet with her two or three times, and every time I would go over there, she would want to fix me lunch, and she would sit down and talk to me and make me feel like I was really special. Right before the next Christmas, we would drag all of those toys out of there, go through them and figure out which ones would work. Then we would take them to places like the Salvation Army and such. It was pretty much just working 18 hours a day for about two weeks.

WELCOME BEAUTIFUL BABY GIRL!

With all of the above nice things that blessed me, the best blessing was the birth of my beautiful, tiny daughter Patricia, on January 12, 1967. "Trish" was born at Bainbridge Naval Hospital and weighed only 3 pounds, 3 ounces. She was in the newborn ICU for two months. You could fit her whole body in your hand, but she has turned into a healthy and beautiful woman.

DELAWARE, PENNSYLVANIA, NEW JERSEY, MARYLAND
JOB: CASUALTY NOTIFICATION

My other two duties included casualty notification, a terrible duty. At that time, the Marine Corp was making notifications on the wounded and also the ones who got killed. The wounded notifications I made by myself.

The area was huge. We had all of Delaware, part of Pennsylvania, part of New Jersey and part of Maryland, so we really kept pretty busy making the notifications.

When people saw me coming, they took it for granted that their son had died. I knew I had to go in into the businesses where people were working. Their company would give me a room where I could talk with them in private.

There were also several incidents where I went to make a call regarding a soldier who had been wounded. One soldier was wounded by being shot in the leg. But as I knocked on the door of the house, I heard the back door slam. As I went around to the back door, the lady came running around the front, and she had her hands over her ears and was running down the street hollering, **"Please don't tell me, please don't tell me, please don't tell me!"** I had to catch her and pull her hands away and tell her that her son was wounded but he was going to be okay. I can remember her hugging me right on that street corner and just bawling her eyes out. She was a really short lady and hid her face in my chest. The whole front of my shirt was wet. It was a terribly emotional job.

I don't know how many death notifications I made. I always went with an officer to make these notifications. I don't know why they always selected me, but I tell you, even today, 50 years later, sometimes I can still visualize us pulling up to the house in that car and walking up the sidewalk to the house. Your heart would always be just pounding in your chest as you knocked on the door, and as soon as they saw you, it was just a horrific scene and then the emotional breakdowns. The Marine's body was normally coming pretty quickly, within a matter of three or four days. So the very day that we made the death notifications, we also had to make funeral arrangements. Normally it was a process where you notified the parents of their son's or daughter's death, and the mourning would probably go on for an hour or two, then we would have to stay and wait until everybody calmed down and then start making some arrangements that very day. That was terrible.

Some of the people took it like they realistically knew the chance of death of their loved one was highly possible. Some of the people had very emotional breakdowns, some with anger; one lady just kept screaming at me, "I wish you was the one who was dead! Why is my son dead? Why ain't you in Vietnam?" She was just angry. She wasn't really angry at me; I was just the messenger. She later apologized to me, and I told her I understood.

I made another notification to a family who were sharecroppers, and their son got killed. For some reason, I made this notification by myself. I went out, and they were all in the field working. I walked out in the field to bring them in, and rode in with them on their wagon and tractor. It was just a very, very spiritual, happy family. I made the notification to them. We always had this document that listed where the soldier was killed and the approximate time of death. The family took the news really well, but then I found out that on that night the son was killed, the mother had a dream where her son came to her and spoke to her, so she knew he was in heaven, and she had relayed that message to her family that morning. When we looked at the death certificate and converted the time from the United States to Vietnam, the time of death was really close to her time of the dream.

There were hundreds of people at the funeral. The church was packed. They had made so many friends, both black and white. I'll never forget them. I spent several visits with them working out the details of the funeral, and I was always invited to share in their meals. They just were a very Christian, loving family. The hardships of being a sharecropper and being poor had no effect on their joy. Their joy was definitely in Christ. This is one of the calls I will never forget.

DELAWARE
JOB: HEAD PALLBEARER

Another responsibility I had was that I was the head pallbearer, so now I was not only making notifications, but it was my job to train the pallbearers. We never wanted the funeral to look routine because we always wanted to make it special; and we practiced—we practiced our walk so we would be in step when we were to carry the casket, we practiced folding the flag which was really what we worried about most because when you fold the flag and it is done, you should just have the blue stars showing, no red at all. Boy, it would be so windy and cold up north in our area that at times you could hardly feel your fingers to fold the flag.

After I folded the flag, I presented it to the officer in charge. He then presented it to the wife or the mother. Then they would play "Taps." I remember watching the wife or mother as they would hold that flag to their breast as if they were holding their husband or son for the last time.

As I watch protestors who disrespect the flag by stepping on it or burning it, I always think about how the fathers, mothers, wives, and children feel that their loved ones who gave their life for their flag and their country. I always think about the veterans who have been seriously wounded, have lost a limb, those who have spent their lives in wheelchairs, and those who live with those dreaded nightmares and flashbacks whose lives will never, ever be normal.....how they must feel as they watch the flag being disrespected, stepped on and burned, when they were willing to give their lives so those who were stepping on the flag and burning it could live in freedom.

SECOND TOUR IN VIETNAM

When my tour was up in Wilmington, Delaware, I received orders to return to Vietnam in September of 1968. I was to be sent to Camp Pendleton, California, for 30 days of physical training before being shipped back out to Vietnam. The 30 days of training were needed to get us back in shape and battle-ready. After a month of hard physical training to snap us into shape, we shipped out to Vietnam.

I was transferred to Northern Vietnam, the Quang Tri province. When I checked in at the base, I met with a captain who went over my records to determine where I should be sent. When he saw I had a Recon MOS (military occupation specialty) he told me he was going to assign me to Third Recon in Da Nang. I told him I already spent one tour in Recon with over 35 missions operating behind enemy lines, and I really didn't want to go back to Recon.

I reasoned that it takes a long time to train a Recon Marine, and there weren't very many Marines trained in Recon left. Now, since there were not enough trained Recon Marines, they were taking top-notch, but unprepared, soldiers and sending them to Recon without any training. Operating behind enemy lines required unique and precise skills. It was scary enough operating behind enemy lines in Viet Cong territory with men who were meticulously trained in the many skills needed to be a Recon Marine and survival skills to operate behind enemy lines.

My arguments weren't getting anywhere with the captain because he recognized the need for someone with my rare MOS and experience. As I sat arguing with him, a lieutenant colonel I served with in the Philippines happened to walk in. He asked where they were sending me. I explained the situation, and he said, "We are really short of platoon sergeants. Go get in the Jeep, and I'll see if I can straighten this out." I got in the Jeep and heard the conversation continue inside the building. The lieutenant colonel came out and said,

"Well, let's go, but they are probably going to come get you in a few days." But they didn't. This is how I wound up in an infantry company as a platoon sergeant of the Third Platoon.

Once I had been introduced to my platoon and talked with them, I was really shocked at both the lapse in training and lack of knowledge that had occurred in the Marine Corps infantry due to the individual rotation. The first time I went to Vietnam, I went with a trained unit. We had trained months together in the United States. We had a solid structure of rank. We had highly trained squad and fire team leaders. But due to the individual rotation, they were sending soldiers to war straight out of boot camp to Vietnam, and through the attrition of casualties, malaria, and rotating home, Marines had moved up through the ranks with no opportunity to be properly trained or gain valuable experience. The only training they received was on the battlefield. They knew little about squad tactics, fire team coordination, artillery fire, or any of that.

In the company, I met a young second lieutenant platoon leader. He possessed no leadership skills. I remember the first thing he said to me was, "Man, I'm glad to see you! I've never had a real platoon sergeant before."

I gathered all the men together and told them of my background in Recon. They were excited and relieved to now finally have an experienced platoon sergeant. They immediately gave me their full confidence. I told them what I expected out of each one of them—in the next few weeks, there would be a lot of changes in their lives and high expectations of them. I then got my squad leaders and fire team leaders together and laid out what I expected of them as leaders, as well as what knowledge and skills they should possess. I let them know if they didn't measure up to these high standards, they would be replaced. They seemed to respond well. Right away, I was impressed with their dedication; I was impressed with how they wanted to change and how they wanted to strive to be the platoon I wanted them to be. I could see, just by my talking to them, they had begun to develop some pride and confidence.

Our company was moving out the very next day. Normally when heading to Vietnam, on account of the heat, we were given two weeks to acclimate to the heat and humidity before being sent into the field, but the company's commander talked to me and said, "This is going to be a major operation. Do you think we can make it without the acclimatizing time? I said, "Sure." For the next week, the sweat ran off of us as we carried 80- or 90-pound loads on our backs in 110 degrees heat. We looked as though we had just stepped out of a swimming pool! We took 22 salt tablets a day plus the malaria pills to survive.

I really don't know how I made it. I bit off more than I could chew, trying to run a platoon and keeping everybody as disciplined and organized as I could. I was totally exhausted; I mean just exhausted from the heat and mental stress. One night I was to lead the men up a little hill to get up to where we were to spend the night, and I remember looking at the base of the hill and thinking this is going to be impossible to climb. I was that exhausted, but I couldn't let the men see how exhausted I was. I had to press on.

We didn't really have any combat on that operation, for which was I was thankful. Next, we were sent to a base camp located in North Vietnam for about a week. In that short week, I held classes on squad tactics, artillery, how to read a map, etc. These are all things they should have known. I drilled them with many different infantry tactics they would need for the survival of the platoon, and they really responded well to improve their skills. The first day we arrived at base camp, they had me send one of my squads out to patrol along the perimeter of the base camp. I could hear their canteens clinking loudly as they walked along, and that was not acceptable for survival. No one taught them how to tie down their equipment or how to move and walk quietly. I taught them how to do this and the importance in doing so.

For the next few weeks, I pushed them hard. A lot of discipline was needed along with instilling confidence in them. Within this time, I saw them grow. They became a unit and very proud of their accomplishments. They knew we were the best in the company and the most organized and knowledgeable. I heard another soldier in another platoon tell one of the men in my platoon, "Man, your sergeant is hard on you. I wouldn't want to be in your platoon." My man said, "No, we really like our sergeant because he is our chance to get home alive." In my first fitness report, my company commander talked about how I gave classes to my men and organized them. He said I had a warehouse full of knowledge. He talked about how I had taken a platoon of young

Marines and turned them into a formidable fighting force in a short period of time.

I really don't remember a lot of my second tour. I guess what happened, as explained by the psychiatrist from the VA (Veterans Administration), is that my mind had blocked a lot of it out. I always have to reference back to my military documents to determine when I was in Vietnam and what battalion and company I was in. They said I was only the second case of anyone who could not remember what company they served or what battalion they were in.

All I can remember is I was the platoon sergeant of the Third Platoon, so I do have some memory, and this is one of my memories of a big operation up along the Cambodian border. There was a huge regimen of Viet Cong from North Vietnam and the North Viet Cong were intense fighters. We expected a tough battle and lots of casualties.

Our bivouac area (a military encampment made with tents) for the night was a large field the Marines had burnt off. They had some tents set up for us to sleep in. The next morning, before the operation, we had a church service. The bivouac was located on top of the hill, and in the valley below, several church services were being held. There were different chaplains of different faiths all holding individual services in that valley.

I was late getting out of the meeting, and the church services had already started. I was on top of the hill, looking down in that valley, and there were a thousand men on their knees. They all had their helmets off, and you could see the lower half of their head was brown and upper half of their head was white where their helmets had blocked the sunlight. I stood there for a minute thinking, "These are some of the toughest men in the world, and they are on their knees asking God for strength." I was a Catholic at that time, and before each battle, we would have a service and the priest would give us absolution.[11]

In this operation, my platoon was in reserve. As we moved out, the ground was just pitted where they had dropped bombs and artillery shells. There were shells and bombs laying all over the place that hadn't exploded, and some of the engineers were carefully picking them up. There were huge stacks of bombs and artillery rounds, probably stacked up 16 to 20 feet square and 4 to 5 feet high. They were going to detonate them in an explosion so the Viet Cong couldn't use them.

As we moved behind a Marine company that we were in reserve for, we came to a hill where the Viet Cong were in spider traps. The spider traps were also ideal for the enemy to pop up, fire and disappear. We were at the base of the hill, as the company we were following was moving up the hill to attack. We were at the bottom of the hill watching the entire fire fight unfold. The Viet Cong would pop out of the spider holes and open fire, forcing

---

[11] Absolution is forgiveness of our sins.

the Marine company to retreat back down the hill. The Marines called in the jet fighters, and the jets would fly in and release rockets. The entire hilltop would be engulfed in one big ball of fire. Then you would hear the explosion. Then we could feel the wave from the heat of the explosion driving past us. We thought surely that must have destroyed most of the Viet Cong. The Marines would start up the hill again, back out of the holes again, the Viet Cong would firing down on them, driving the Marines back down the hill. We watched in horror as the Marine casualties mounted up from the battle. The Marines called in more jets and more rockets, and the same thing; the whole hilltop would be engulfed in a ball of fire, a massive explosion, and we could feel the wave of heat from the concussion drive past us. After about the third or fourth time, the Marines were finally able to take the hill. We watched as they dug the Viet Cong out of the spider traps and bunkers and wiped them out. It was a helpless and horrible feeling to watch our fellow Marines die as they fought hard to take the hill and we weren't allowed to help them. The horror of these experiences will be forever embedded in my memory until the day God takes me home.

Once a month we would go back to the Quang Tri Province, which was our base camp. We would get new clothes and socks. They had cold showers set up. It would be the only shower we had taken in a month. We always took 22 salt tablets a day, and our clothes would be white from sweating out salt. We would take all our clothes off on one side of the showers and throw them in a big pile. Then we would brush our teeth, take our showers, and exit on the other side. At the exit, there were huge stacks of fresh, clean clothes, we would sort through to find our sizes.

From there, we went down to the clubs, the enlisted club, the NCO (noncommissioned officer) club, and the officers' club, depending on our rank. We were craving cold drinks after not having any for a month. I remember we would get pretty loaded on cold beer. It tasted so good!

The next morning, we packed up and went back out again. This particular time, they were going to sweep an area which had hardly ever had any Viet Cong in the area before. They were there this time. An intense fire fight ensued, and the first wave of Marines went in. As we awaited our turn, I was lying on the ground trying to get a few more moments of sleep, still pretty hung over from the previous night of drinking. I had my helmet covering my face, and I fell fast asleep. I was sleeping pretty soundly, when somebody came by and started kicking me. I was quite aggravated, and I said in a loud voice, "You kick me one more time, and I'm going to get up and kick your ass all over this hillside." Everything got deathly quiet. Men had been talking, but now, silence prevailed all around me, and I thought, "What's going on?"

I sat up, pushing my helmet back, and there standing before me was a two-star general looking right at me, as well as the battalion sergeant major. I was stunned, shocked, and embarrassed. I tried to jump up to salute, but I had about an 80-pound pack on my back, and all I could do was fall back to the ground. The general said, "Take it easy Sarge, just take it easy." He sat down and spent about 15 to 20 minutes just talking to me, asking me how it was going and where I was from, and how my men were doing. He was really interested in our welfare. He said, "Well, the sergeant major and I are going out to check and see if they got the Viet Cong cleaned up yet."

They loaded on a chopper and went out for a look. A little while later, he came back and sat down and talked to me again. He said, "It looks like they're about to wrap things up out there. You guys will be heading out soon. Take care of yourself."

It wasn't too long after that operation we moved back to a base called LZ Stud, which I have mentioned before. We were there for about a week, and one morning we heard this jet aircraft flying over, with its engine sputtering. We looked up, and saw a pilot eject from the plane and parachute into the LZ Stud base. He had been in North Vietnam where his plane was hit, and he limped it back to LZ Stud. We watched the plane fly another 3 miles before it hit and exploded into the top of a mountain. Shortly after the crash, the company commander called me down to headquarters and said to take my platoon to the crash site to make sure the radio equipment and the rest of the classified equipment on the plane are destroyed. The mountainside was extremely steep and rugged with loose rocks.

We left early the next morning. We hiked about 45 minutes, and when we arrived at the base of the mountain, we prepared to climb a steep, nearly vertical slope. I had to hold my men against parts of the steep cliff walls, and push them up over several inclines. Some of the inclines necessitated that we remove our packs, latch them to ropes, and pull them up and over the inclines. The ropes were then tied off and secured so the men could pull themselves up and over the same inclines. Once we got to the top of the mountain, we quickly located the crash site. The jet was completely destroyed on impact. There was nothing left. We verified that the radio and other equipment were completely destroyed on impact as well.

We started back down the mountain, and there was one spot that was a sheer cliff with an 8-foot drop. We would lower each other down by one man hanging on to the hands of a man above him as he slid down to a very narrow ledge. The cliff dropped off again. I was standing on the second narrow ledge, hanging on to a tree, and holding the men against the cliff until they could gain their footing before moving horizontally off the ledge to safe ground.

I was holding one of the men against the cliff, and the man who lowered him accidentally kicked a big rock loose. The rock was at least 18 inches round. It came down and hit him right on the side of the head and knocked him out for a time. I held onto him until I got help to slide him off of the ledge and let him down. He had a pack on his back with two cans of machine gun ammo weighing about 30 pounds total. I knew he was done for or severely injured. We got him up, he was conscious, but he could barely walk.

I needed to disperse his ammo, and I found one man who had enough room on his pack to strap on one can of the machine gun ammo. I strapped the other can to my pack. I now had three cans of machine gun ammo and two 60 mm mortar rounds strapped to my pack. I had over 100 pounds on my back and I needed to help the injured man the rest of the way down the mountain. He was barely conscious and having a hard time walking. At times I had to carry the full weight of his body with his feet dragging the ground. It was tough and slow going, but we made it to the bottom of the mountain. As we approached the perimeter of the LZ we had to walk through a clearing, when a few Viet Cong opened fire on us. We began running as fast as we could towards some trenches. I was running with the injured man, holding on to his upper body with one arm and the seat of his pants with my other hand so we could move along as fast as we could to get into the trenches.

Normally the trenches weren't very deep, so I thought they would be really shallow.

I wasn't paying attention as we both jumped over the side of a trench to find the trench to be 6 feet deep. Down I went with the force of all 100 plus pounds on my back. When I hit the bottom, both of my ankles buckled underneath me. I severely sprained both of them really severe. They swelled up almost instantaneously. I did make it back to the outpost LZ Stud, and I was there for a couple of days. My ankles were so bruised and swollen, I could barely get my boots on.

For support, the corpsman had to tightly wrap both my ankles.

A few days later, we started off on another operation. I was still having a lot of pain in both my ankles. My ankles were so weak, while walking through the jungle they would twist and turn sideways at least two or three times a day; I had no strength left in them. This went on for maybe a week, and they got so bad I could feel my ankle bones slipping in and out. One evening one of my ankles swelled up big and puffy, and turned black, and I couldn't get my boot on at all. The medics knew they had to Medivac me out, but it was the dark of night and they would have to wait until morning for the chopper to pick me up.

The next morning, the medics flew me out, and they dropped me off in this huge open field where there were 40 other casualties lying under a large tree. I guess we were waiting for a bigger helicopter or something to transport us to the hospital. I still had my rifle, grenades, and ammo.

This doctor came by and asked me, "Sarge, you got any pain?" I was in tremendous pain. My whole ankle had turned black. I said, "Yeah, I'm in quite a bit of pain." So he gave me something for pain. He came back again a short time later, and I think he forgot who I was since he was looking after so many wounded. He was just jumping from man-to-man and trying to do his best until they could get them on a chopper and transport the wounded men to a hospital. Then he came by again and said, "Got any pain?" I said, "Yes." So he gave me something else. It wasn't long before all my pain went away. I didn't have any pain at all, so I got up and walked around a little bit, and I thought, "Well, heck, I'm okay." I had taken so much medication, I thought I could walk just fine, but really not fine at all.

I thought, "Well, I'll just go back to my outfit." I couldn't get my boot on one of my feet, so I tied my boot on the back of my pack, and I started walking down the road with one boot on and one boot off. Three men came running out before me, and they kept circling me. They asked, "Where are you going Sarge?" I said, "Well, I'm okay now. I'm going to go on back to my outfit." Then one of the men convinced me by saying, "They're just going to take you over to the hospital and put a cast on your foot; you'll probably go on back to your outfit tomorrow." I said, "Well, that's okay." They sat me down, and they took all my ammo, grenades, and rifle.

I was finally taken to a hospital and became violently ill the next morning. I don't know what that doctor gave me, but it likely was a double dose of morphine which sure messed me up for a couple of days. They did put casts on both of my legs and told me my tour was done, and I was being transported to the U.S. Army Hospital in Japan.

A COMBAT PLATOON SERGEANT'S JOB

Being a platoon sergeant in peacetime was not a bad job. It allowed time to train my men. But in wartime, the task was nightmarish, and I somehow knew I could never prepare them well enough to get everybody home alive. Some of the men in my platoon would likely be killed or wounded, and I would forever blame myself since they were in my charge. I would carry the scars of the memories of the men I lost for the rest of my life. Thoughts would torment, "If only I had done things differently" or "only if I had been better."

I was a good platoon sergeant, and my men looked up to me. I could not help but get really emotionally close. I always ran a very disciplined platoon and put my men's needs before my own without exception. Any time that we were in base camp in Vietnam, where we could get a hot meal, clothing, supplies, medical care, etc., I would always make sure the men got their supplies before I did. I made sure of all of this before I took care of my own needs. This is how we trained in the Marine Corps—to always attend to our men's needs before our own. I was close to my men. I was tough on them, but they respected me for that. They knew I wanted to get as many of them home as possible.

Once, we were back in base camp for a day, and some of the men came down to the noncommissioned officers' club to tell me they were not allowed into the enlisted men's club to drink beer, and they asked me if I could go over and talk to the club manager. I said "sure." I stood toe-to-toe with a sergeant major in a yelling contest, holding up for my men, even though the sergeant major was threatening me with a court martial if I didn't leave the area. I didn't leave the area, and I didn't back down, even though I was scared of getting court martialed, busted of my rank, and thereby possibly being unable to even feed my family.

In war, I expected the men to do their job, even if it cost them their lives; so, as a sergeant, I had to stand up for them when somebody else did them wrong, even if it cost me my rank or to be court martialed.

As their sergeant, I was always aware of my men's mental attitudes and noticed when they may be reaching a flash point or mental breakdown. I could recognize if one of my men needed moved back to the rear or sent home for mental help. Having a man fall apart in war or on the battlefield can get a lot of men killed.

Sometimes men received upsetting letters from home—their wife had moved on and wanted a divorce; their parents were diagnosed with a fatal disease, and so on and so forth. Emotional duress could stem from any number of factors and I always wanted to keep an open line of communication with my men. I wanted them to know I would do anything in my power to help them when they were facing tough problems. The downside of this is that they felt comfortable enough to tell me their hopes and dreams, show me pictures from home of their children, wives, girlfriends, dogs, or cars. Many times they would read me their letters from home. This personal relationship was not good for me because knowing their personal life just made it harder when I lost someone. Additional combat didn't necessarily toughen me up; it began to wear me down and left us all wondering how much more we could possibly take.

The men in the platoon thought I was fearless. They called me "Sergeant Rock." If they only knew, behind the tough face and the firm, confident voice barking orders, I was just as scared as they were. I remember a time when we were going into an area where we expected to see some heavy combat, and one of the men came up to me and said, "Sarge, I'm scared, I'm really scared." I tried to comfort him and told him he was going to be alright, telling him, "You'll be alright, we'll get through this, we'll get through it." Then he looked at me and said, "I wish, I wish I was like you; you're not scared of anything." I was thinking "If he only knew I was just as scared as he was." I prayed this prayer many times: "God, I'm not asking you to spare my life, but I'm asking you to give me the courage to get through this day. If my courage should fail me, Lord, please don't let me leave this battlefield alive because you know I could never face my men, my family, or ever face myself. I'm asking you, Lord, if my courage fails me, do not let me leave this battlefield alive."

That night I was injured, and they were going to medivac me out in the morning. The men kept asking me if I would be back and who would take over the platoon if I didn't return. No one else had the expertise needed to lead them. They were scared, they were VERY scared. They were especially scared because we had a major operation coming up and there would likely be some heavy combat.

The next morning, I was lifted from the battlefield by helicopter. Once in the air, I began thinking, "I am going to live to see my children." Little did I know that these words were going to haunt me for the rest of my life. Two weeks later, while I was at the Naval Hospital in Memphis, Tennessee, I learned that the platoon was ambushed and most of the men were killed. I had a guilty feeling—because I felt I was being selfish thinking about seeing my family and being able to live when I should have been worrying about the platoon and who was going to be leading it. Today, I still suffer with survivor's guilt and the feeling that I put myself first instead of the welfare of the platoon.

I was so angry that I swore that day I would go to hell before I would ever bow or kneel before a god who didn't allow me to be with my men when they were ambushed or even allow me to die with them. Even though I was in the hospital due to an injury I received in Vietnam at the time my platoon was ambushed, I still, to this day, carry a lot of guilt and blame over what happened to them.

There was an officer, a platoon leader, whose name was Lieutenant McIntosh. He was a very young second lieutenant. He had no experience in leadership, nor had he ever been in infantry. He was a good guy, but the men didn't have any confidence in him, and he was always telling me, "Sarge, you're too hard on the men." However, because I was an experienced combat veteran, I ran the platoon until I was injured. At that point, Lieutenant McIntosh was naturally the one to take over the platoon since he was an officer.

The day I was medically discharged from the Marines at the base in Quantico, Virginia, I stopped by the hobby shop to pick up something I had made; I don't remember what it was. While I was there, I ran into Lieutenant McIntosh. He had survived the ambush. He had been shot in the face during the battle. He could not look at me directly; he just kept looking at the ground and saying it was horrible. I looked into his eyes; they were set and dull, and I could feel the pain he was suffering. He lamented letting the platoon become lax and undisciplined and knew now I was right about pushing them hard for their own survival. I feel sorry for him to this day, and I wonder if he is still alive. War is really tough, and I somehow knew I needed to be tough on my men.

It gets so hot in Vietnam, we would be carrying 80 or 90 pounds on our back, and the temperature would make it as high as 120 degrees. We would sweat profusely— so much that it poured off of us like we just got out of the swimming pool. We could not wear underwear because it would get soaked and sweaty and wad up. Men would get so tired after a few days on the move, they would let their guard down. Sometimes they would get so tired, they hardly cared whether they lived or died. It was especially in these times of complete exhaustion that I kept pushing and pushing my men.[12] The Viet Cong were experts at keeping us awake all night long by dropping mortar rounds every 30 minutes or so. If we were attacked and didn't have our perimeters set up, we could get a lot of men killed.

This was one of the problems I saw in my second tour. A large percentage of all those deaths were due to a lack of discipline because there were no experienced platoon sergeants left.

I still blame myself for what happened to the platoon. For 50 years, even though I was not in the battle, I would still have daytime flashbacks as if I was there when they were being attacked. I could hear the gunfire; I could hear the screams of the men who were being shot. It would be so real it almost felt like it was happening at that moment all over again, and the flashbacks would last for hours.

---

[12] *Thank you, Patty Black, for explaining to all of us what "exhausted" really means and how loosely so many of us use that term, not realizing how our military suffered through pushing their limits so we could remain free.*

A STORY ABOUT A YOUNG
MARINE SQUAD LEADER

We were in a small outpost called LZ[13] Stud. LZ Stud was located in North Vietnam. We were surrounded by Viet Cong. It was an inhumane and terribly depressing place. Rats were as big as cats, and at night you could hear them dragging their tails as they ran around the edges of the bunkers. The bunkers were pretty much in the open, so we were in the hot sun all day long.

There was a was a small airfield at LZ Stud, and the Viet Cong would shell the base every day. They would drop rockets and mortars on us, and they would probe the perimeter of our line causing small fire fights all night long to keep us awake. Thankfully we never had a major attack— just aggravation and sleep deprivation.

My whole platoon consisted of three individual squads and each squad was

---

[13] In military terminology a landing zone (LZ) is an area where aircraft can land.

manning a remote outpost. Each outpost was about a mile from the main base. The outposts were there in case of an attack on the main base. They would be the first to be in contact with the enemy—kind of a sacrificial position. There were probably only seven or eight men at each outpost. They had bunkers at each outpost for their protection. I didn't see the men every day. Some of the men in each squad would come back to LZ Stud to pick up supplies and go back to their outpost. One day, some of the men from the first squad arrived and said their squad leader, Corporal Clark, had malaria and was sweating and shaking at night. There was no way we could travel up there at night, so a corpsman and I caught a Jeep the next morning and went up to check on Corporal Clark. We didn't have any thermometers because it got so hot in Vietnam that thermometers would just bust. We talked to Corporal Clark, and he said it was just something he ate and he was feeling fine. While we were there, he looked well enough, and I guess that's how malaria just kind of comes and goes.

The next day we got our orders to move out. We were going to move north out of LZ Stud to attack a large Viet Cong stronghold. It was near the Cambodian border. We were loaded up and ready to head out. The corpsman got some medical supplies which included some thermometers. I told him, "Before we head out, why don't you take Corporal Clark's temperature?" The corpsman took his temperature, and it read 106 degrees; he had full-blown malaria. I said to him, "Corporal Clark, we have to get you to the hospital. You know, at 106 degrees, you could have brain damage." He said, "But Sarge, you know where we are going. We're probably going to get in a fire fight, and the others in my squad lack experience, so I gotta go; I've got to be with my squad." He was adamant! We had to force him to the ground. There was an ice house there, and we got a block of ice. We took his shirt off and rubbed ice on his back, trying to bring his temperature down while waiting for a medivac helicopter to come in and pick him up. I'll never forget looking back as we were moving out towards the loading zone, and seeing him sitting on the ground with his head between his legs, crying. He thought he was letting his men down. I lost contact with him but have often wondered how he did and whether or not he suffered any brain damage? He was just 19 years old.

There are many other veterans like Corporal Clark, unsung heroes of the Vietnam war, with amazing stories of patriotism and self-sacrifice.

CHRISTMAS IN VIETNAM

I have some good memories of Vietnam, including a very special Christmas in 1967. We had endured several terrible weeks on the battlefield. Our platoon was 30 men when we started, and we were down to 13, though not all were casualties of war. Some of the men rotated home, and we lost quite a few to malaria. We actually lost more men to malaria than battle.

It was late Christmas Eve when we arrived at our base camp. There was not going to be any Christmas meal for us. Our Christmas meal would be our C-rations. Christmas in a war zone was very depressing with thoughts about all we were missing—home, the Christmas meal, church, opening presents, and family get-togethers. We were all mentally down and wondering if any of us would possibly live to see another Christmas.

As a platoon sergeant, I always tried to hide my emotions. When we got to base camp, I was exhausted. I was homesick and wondering if I would ever again see my children. And I also wondered who would come into their lives if I was killed—would they be loved or mistreated? I felt I was going to have an emotional breakdown, but as a platoon sergeant, I knew I could not give into my feelings in front of my men, so I found a spot away from everyone. I sat against a tree, and I began crying. I told God, "I don't want this job anymore. I don't want to be responsible for the lives of the men in this platoon."

Being a platoon sergeant is a sacrificial job. Being a leader of any type is a sacrificial job. I just didn't want to be responsible anymore for their lives. I was 26 years old at this time. I heard my name called. It was a Marine who had been looking for us for hours as he had mail for the platoon. I received a box of cookies from home which had been shipped about four weeks earlier. The box had busted open, and the cookies were stale and covered with red ants. But that was all we had, and that was going to be our Christmas treat.

As we sat in a circle, knocking off those ants and eating the stale cookies, one of the Marines asked: "If I don't make it, would one of you guys go by and see my mom? I know she is going to take it really hard if I don't make it home. Would you tell her I loved her?" One of the Marines said, "If I make it, I'll go by and tell her." Another Marine said, " My daughter was only a few months old when I left home. She doesn't know me. If I don't make it home, would somebody contact her, keep in touch with her, and when she gets old enough, tell her I was a good Marine?"

Phone numbers and addresses were exchanged and commitments made to comfort, visit and look after the families of those Marines who didn't make it home. We told stories of past Christmases until late into the night. Of all of the Christmases I have lived through, this is a most special Christmas memory. We had no material gifts to exchange, but we had better gifts— those of love and devotion to each other.

Every Christmas, I visualize sitting on that foxhole, and I imagine a glow around us. I know that God was there with us that night as we gave the only gifts we had—the promise to pass on a message of the fallen soldier to his family. You hear about camaraderie on the battlefield. It's a close relationship with fellow soldiers where everything is shared. The phrase "I got your back" means "I'll give my life before I'll let my brothers or sisters down." We don't pray on the battlefield to spare our lives— we pray for the courage to do our jobs, just as Jesus did in the Garden of Gethsemane.

A GIFT OF SPIRITUAL AWAKENING

It's been over 50 years ago, and I cherish that Christmas memory still; it is truly special. God sent Jesus into this world on Christmas with the gift of our salvation, no material gifts. The story of the crucifixion and the reason for our salvation is summed up in John 3:16: *"For God gave the world his only begotten son, and whosoever believes in him shall not perish but shall have everlasting life."* Jesus is the reason for the Christmas season, but is rarely offered gifts. He doesn't care about the material world, but appreciates gifts of time and service to the kingdom of God.

Christmas in Vietnam helped me consider the gifts that matter most: the gift of joy that comes from meeting the needs of another, the gift of befriending a lost soul, the gift of comforting someone in a nursing home or Veterans' home. Then there is the gift of overcoming addictions of greed, selfishness, and materialism to become a better father or mother or spouse. There are gifts of service to churches and communities—these are the gifts that God appreciates and the best things to offer to Jesus who gave us the ultimate gift of our salvation.

Every Christmas, I visualize sitting on that foxhole, and I imagine a glow around us. I know that God was there with us that night as we gave the only gifts we had—the promise to pass on a message of the fallen soldier to his family.

ANGELS OF MERCY/US ARMY HOSPITAL 106, JAPAN

I met some of the greatest heroes when I was injured in my second tour in Vietnam—nurses caring for the wounded. I was sent to US Army hospital 106 in Japan, where I spent about 10 days in the orthopedic ward. Even though I had seen some horrifying things on the battlefield, I was not mentally prepared for what I witnessed in that ward.

There were at least 30 men in that ward, many were missing both hands, some were missing both hands and both legs, all on that ward had some combination of missing limbs. I was the only one that had both my hands and legs.

For the next 10 days, I watched in amazement as Angels (the nurses), with hearts like Jesus, took care of these men. They tenderly fed the men with no hands; they took time out from their busy day to read them their letters from home; they wrote letters for them; they cleaned their terrible wounds; they took time from their busy day to visit and encourage them. Some of the men were so deeply depressed they wanted to die. The nurses would stay after their shift was over and come up with games to play with these men to get their minds off their deep depression. The nurses helped fit new artificial legs on men that had one or both legs amputated, and they would celebrate as these men took their first steps on their new legs.

I remember thinking we combat soldiers may see some combat once or twice a month, but these nurses are in a battle every day - they get no breaks. We now see the toll that the job has taken on these nurses, many have severe cases of PTSD.

Women have been taking care of wounded soldiers as far back as the civil war; most then were local volunteers with little or no training. I have read stories told by civil war soldiers who witnessed it firsthand. Women from local villages would hear the cries of the wounded, or learn of wounded and dying men who needed cared for. Some such women were even seen on the battlefield, the gunfire raging around them, attending to the wounded and dying. The caring and nurturing spirit those women had made them oblivious to the battle around them. Some lost their lives. The soldiers called them the Angels of Mercy.

Seven thousand women served as nurses in World War II. I read a story about a hospital in France during World War II that was being shelled by the Germans. There was no time to evacuate the wounded soldiers; they told the nurses to evacuate the hospital, but the nurses refused to leave. Several nurses died that day shielding a wounded soldier with their own bodies as artillery shells came through the roof of that hospital.

Grace Newton was a World War II nurse and relates this story: "I can't forget one young soldier whose bravery collapsed in a last desperate cry as the medical officer walked away unable to save him. The soldier said to me, 'Nurse, don't let me die.' Kneeling beside his cot, all I could do was to hold him as he died. What little we had to offer—sometimes only a prayer that God would bring a quick death."

Alice Lofgren said, "No matter how sad or bad the wound, the nurse always knew that her job was to make the men feel better, even if her own heart was breaking." She said, "These women loved their patients, and their hearts ached when they couldn't save a life or relieve suffering. Their hearts ache even today."

US ARMY HOSPITAL 106 HEROES
TAKE A BREAK

While I was still in the hospital in the orthopedic ward, I could get around, so I met some other Marines. There were two Marines that I met on another ward. They had been wounded pretty severely. They had casts on both their arms and legs. They were in the same outfit, and when an artillery exploded, it got both of them. They had about 200 to 300 stitches in them. They were lucky they didn't bleed to death. On the same ward, there was a gunnery sergeant who had lost a leg in Vietnam. He was kind of a crazy guy. None of us had been afforded liberty for a long time and we had been living in miserable conditions in Vietnam. But there was a club on the base in Japan where the hospital was located. I was delegated to persuade the head nurse to let us go down to the club. She gave us permission to go down for a couple of hours. Little did she know that sending four Marines in the direction of booze and women could cause major trouble!

We got a wheelchair for the gunnery sergeant, and we started down towards the club. These guys could barely walk; I don't know how long it took us to get to the club, they were stoked up from all the shrapnel they had in them. We got to the club and were told to leave the wheelchair in a designated area, take the gunnery sergeant over to a table, get him on a chair, and afterward, we could get the wheelchair again.

So we got to drinking! We had been living out in the war zone and where it was very hot. We desired anything cold and also hadn't partied in a long time, so it didn't take long for us to down a few beers and get pretty buzzed up. I'm telling you, the gunnery sergeant could hop on that one leg like a rabbit, so he started getting up and hopping around. He would hop out to the dance floor and just stand out there wobbling around. A couple of times the club manager told me to get him to sit back down. I got him and sat him down. The more he drank, the harder he was to control.

They had a little country western band when we got there. It was comprised of four Japanese girls. They were pretty good singers. The next act was some GoGo girls. The gunnery sergeant started hopping around again, and then the club manager came over and told me to go get him off the dance floor. I think they were worried about him falling down. We were all getting pretty drunk. So I went looking for the gunnery sergeant and finally found him. As I was taking him back to the table, I looked up to see the other two guys (pictured), with all their casts, dancing with the GoGo girls up onstage! By this time, the owners of the club had enough of us. They told me to go get the wheelchair, put the gunnery sergeant in it and get the hell out of there!

We got a pretty good buzz on, and would have liked to have stayed longer;

however, they kicked us out, and we had to go back to the ward. The next day we were written up in a report, so that was the end of our liberty; we weren't allowed back to that club anymore!

LAST DAYS IN THE MARINES

NAVAL HOSPITAL IN MEMPHIS, TENNESSEE

I was transferred from the Army Hospital 106 in Japan to the naval hospital in Memphis, Tennessee, for further evaluation by the orthopedic department. They were going to keep me there for some daily physical therapy. They tested the movement of my ankles, and there was 4 degrees more movement than there should have been. This was because my ligaments were badly stretched.

Since I was a staff sergeant, I was in charge of keeping the ward clean. Every week they would have an inspection to see who had the cleanest ward. For five weeks in a row I got the award for the cleanest ward. So at six weeks, the nurse said, "Bob, we still have the cleanest ward, but ward 6 has done a really good job, and since we won it five weeks in a row, they are asking if it would be okay to give ward 6 the recognition." I said, "Yeah, that's fine."

I stayed for another two weeks, and I won the award the next two weeks in a row. I got a fitness report from that nurse. On the fitness report, she told the story that I won the award five weeks in a row and then they gave it to another ward, but we really had the cleanest ward.

QUANTICO/MOON & BELINDA
AND THE MARINE CORPS BALL

I was then transferred to the rifle range at Quantico, Virginia. I was on limited duty. I couldn't do much. I was there for four months, and I went to physical therapy every morning to see if I could gain any strength back in my ankles before an evaluation by the medical board.

I was in charge of the indoor pistol range where the Marine rifle and pistol team were stationed. When they were in town, they would practice there, and I would operate the automated targets for them and assist the practice. I ran NRA matches at the indoor pistol range, and I got paid $25 for that, which was pretty good money.

Every morning we had a company formation, and I was in charge of all of the coaches for the outdoor rifle ranges. This particular morning, all I had to do was come in and give my morning report, and I was off for the rest of the day, so I thought I would take my two children with me. My son Joe was 4 years old at this time, and my daughter Trish was 3 years old. As I was getting ready to give my morning report to the company commander, I heard this voice calling for me, "Dad, Dad!" As I looked out of the corner of my eye, I could see Joe leading Trish down the sidewalk towards our formation, and he said, "Dad, Trish has gotta go pee." You could hear laughter throughout the company. The company commander could barely contain himself, but he did say, "Sergeant Gannon, it looks like you've got a problem you need to take care of. You are dismissed." I did a sharp military right turn and marched off.

On Wednesday nights, the Marines and their families could come in and shoot, so I stayed late. There was an officer candidate training program at Quantico where the Marines trained their officers. If an officer couldn't qualify with a pistol, then he would be dropped from the Marine Corps. The ones who were having trouble qualifying would be sent to the indoor pistol range, and I would work to help them qualify so they could stay in the program.

We lived in a trailer court in Quantico, Virginia. Right across the road from us lived a Marine, named Moon Mullets, and his wife. Moon was nothing but skin and bones. He was just *skinny*. His wife Belinda probably weighed about 240 LBS or something like that; she was a big girl. They were both drinkers. They spent most of their money on booze. They invited me over to their trailer a couple of times, and the trailer was a wreck. The curtains were hanging off the windows. They had holes in the walls from when they would get in a drunken fight. One night they invited one of her friends over, and Moon and Belinda got in a fight. Belinda threw a can of beer at Moon, and it missed him but hit her friend in the head and knocked her out. They had to get the ambulance out there to revive her.

Periodically they would give up drinking and get religion. They would get all dressed up for a week or two and go to church. They hadn't bought the kids Sunday clothes for a long time, and the first morning I saw them going to church, the kids looked like they were going wading in the water. Their pants were about 3 or 4 inches too short, and their arms stuck way out of their jacket sleeves. They did the best they could. That religion would last maybe for a week or two, and then they would be back at it.

Every year the Marines had a Marine Corps Ball, and the event was formal. We would go in our Marine dress blues, and the women would also get all dressed up. Belinda went to the thrift store and found this big yellow gown. I can't describe it; it was huge and had a hat with a veil hanging down. She put that thing on and showed us all. She was really proud of it. Their car broke down, so they needed a ride to the Marine Corps Ball. I said, "Yeah, you can ride with us." So when we got there, Moon and Belinda went in and sat with their company, and I sat with my company. She stood out on the dance floor in that big yellow formal gown she had on. She could be spotted all over the place, and she was dancing with all kinds of men. I wondered if Moon would become jealous. Soon after, I saw Moon in his dress blues, heading out to the dance floor. I knew there was going to be trouble. They got in an argument and started fist fighting on the dance floor. She was big enough that she held her own. She threw a punch and hit Moon right in the nose, and his nose started bleeding. Since he started the fight, they threw him out and left her in there.

It was cold that night. I was still inside enjoying the evening with my company when one of the event planners told me Moon was outside wanting to talk to me. I went outside and found him sitting with a bloody nose, leaning against a post out by the front door. He was catching the blood in his white Marine Corps hat. He said, "I need to go home." I was pretty upset with him and said, "I'll tell you what, I'm not taking you home. You need to find a ride with somebody else. I'm having a good time. You started the trouble, and you can just sit out here in the cold for all I care." I think he got a ride home with somebody else. They were a pretty odd couple and quite unforgettable!

MEDICAL DISCHARGE FROM THE MARINES

After four months of physical therapy at Quantico, I went before the medical board. The doctors on that board told me the only recourse for the ankle injuries I had sustained would be surgery to cut and shorten my ligaments. This option would most likely cause a loss of flexibility in my feet so it wasn't recommended. I refused the procedure. They would temporarily retire me on account of my time in the service. I would have three years to try to overcome that injury, and I would go for a physical evaluation every year.

Shortly afterwards, I received my medical discharge. It was pretty traumatic for me because the service had been my life. I had never succeeded in anything else. After feeling worthless all those growing up years, I had done so well as a Recon Marine, I had made staff sergeant in six years, I was almost qualified for a promotion to gunnery sergeant which is E7 (the highest rank an enlisted man can accomplish would be E9), a sergeant major. It was a very sad day, and I remember thinking, "God, here we go again. Now what am I going to do? I don't have any skills. I've got nothing."

I knew my best avenue would be to go to college, but I had a very limited education and being in special ed does not boost your ego or confidence. I felt I had no choice. Just like in the Marines, I had to **NEVER GIVE UP**. I knew I had to maintain that Recon attitude to achieve my goals in life!

MAPPING OUT MY LIFE AFTER DISCHARGE
FROM THE MARINES

The day I was discharged from the Marines was depressing. I had 9 years, 4 months, and 22 days—almost 10 years in the Marine Corps. I made rank fast, yet here I was, starting over again. I was thinking, "God, **WHY, WHY** have you done this to me?"

I loved the Marine Corps. It was a very hard life. War was tough, but it was where I found my dignity, pride, and sense of accomplishment. It was who I was. After growing up in a dysfunctional atmosphere with a learning disability, I had achieved a lot in the Marine Corps. And now, here I was—no desire to work in a factory, no real job opportunities, and no education except for the meager schooling I'd received in special ed.

I decided I had to go to college. I wanted a job that offered the same sense of accomplishment that I had in the Marine Corps—a job that was both enjoyable and lucrative. I never wanted to relive those degrading feelings I had as a child convincing me that I was a loser.

So, I started checking into some colleges and chose Linn Technical College in Linn, Missouri. I was impressed when I visited the school and talked with the recruiters. I decided I was going to study electronics. I fully expected to fail some courses. I knew that I didn't have much of an education. I took the entrance exams, and I tested with a sixth-grade education level. I also flunked the electronics exam, but they saw something in me and decided to let me take the electronics course.

I told my parents I was going to Linn Tech to study electronics. Of course, my dad responded negatively, "I don't know why you are taking electronics; you are too dumb. You'll never make it." This was the same thing he told me when I joined the Marine Corps. He said, "The Marine Corps is a tough place. You'll never make it." But now, I was different. I had achieved. I had become a Recon Marine. I was one of the prestigious less-than-one-percent who had achieved the honor of being a Recon Marine!

I became a platoon sergeant at 24 years of age. I survived 35 missions behind enemy lines. I led 25 missions as a platoon sergeant in my first tour. In my second tour, I was recognized for my knowledge and leadership skills, and no longer would I allow anybody to discourage my dream.

I knew I would achieve and accomplish this goal, even though I had a great obstacle to overcome—a sixth-grade education level. I knew <u>I could only truly fail if I quit, and quitting was no longer in my vocabulary. Anybody can be a quitter; it takes no talent.</u>

Staying the course in the face of adversity not only fosters self-confidence, it allows others to share in that sense of pride too. Children, family and neighbors are inspired when they can clearly witness struggles overcome by determination and perseverance. It becomes an example for everyone watching. So, I wasn't about to let the possibility of a failed class prevent me from moving forward. I didn't care. I knew now, no matter what, I would accomplish my goal and graduate from Linn Tech.

LINN TECH AND ME AND MY OLD TRUCK

I only had $600 when I got out of the Marines. There were no jobs in Linn, Missouri, at all. Linn was a remote town. So, I took my $600, and bought an old '52, 2-ton flatbed truck and a chainsaw. The truck was really beat up. The window on the driver's side was gone. There was no heater. I could see the road beneath me through holes in the floorboard as I was driving! No matter how cold it was, after loading three cords of wood on that truck, I would be sweating. Since I had no heat, I carried five blankets with me. As I started down the road, and I started cooling off, I started wrapping those blankets around me to stay warm. There was a constant draft in that truck because of the holes in the floor.

I didn't have a window on the driver's side; I had a piece of cardboard I would hold up to the window hole to try to block some of the cold air. When I turned left, I had to take the cardboard down.

I went back to doing the only thing I knew how to do which was cut cord wood. In those days, we got $9.00 per cord. A cord of wood was 4 feet high, 4 feet wide, and 8 feet long. The wood was cut, split and loaded on the truck, hauled, and unloaded in the charcoal kiln. It was tough, and I barely eked out a living. I would cut three cords of wood a day on weekends, and in the summertime when I wasn't going to school, I would cut wood every day.

I moved my family into an old farmhouse and agreed to work out my rent.

The landlord was going to charge me $45 per month. The farmhouse was a wreck. It was full of rats of mice. We all slept in one room because we could hear the rats running across the ceiling at night, and everybody was afraid. We had to wash dishes before we ate because mice were running over almost anything in the house. I didn't have any income at that time besides what I made cutting cord wood. We lived in that farmhouse for four months. Then I got my schooling benefits from the military, which was $125 a month, and we moved out to a trailer which was quite a bit better. At least we didn't have any mice or rats running around.

I started school, and it was really tough. The first class was Algebra I. With a sixth-grade education, I didn't even know about positive and negative numbers. What saved me was that I had the same group of people in all of my classes and became acquainted with classmates who were able to help me with my homework.

My first year I had Algebra I, Algebra II, Trigonometry, along with the basic required courses. My second year, I had to take Physics, Analytic Geometry and Calculus. It was a very hard struggle. The people at Linn Tech knew my unique situation and educational background, and the whole staff and administration were always encouraging me.

My schedule was harrowing. I took that 2-ton truck to school, and when we got out at 3 o'clock, I headed for the woods. I cut wood until dark, and then I would try to find a study group or classmates who could tutor me. I would usually study until 2 or 3 o'clock in the morning. I didn't sleep much in those days, in part, because I had a very serious case of posttraumatic stress. But mostly, those sleep deficits were the result of the new battle I was in to make the grade at college. Every quarter when we got our report cards; I was always anxious to see if I passed all my courses.

Those were some very tough years. One time, I was totally discouraged. I had no money. I was completely exhausted from cutting wood, attending school, and struggling to make grades because I was far behind. I decided I just couldn't hang on any longer. I bought a six-pack of really cheap beer. It tasted terrible, but I took it to the woods. I was lying against the wheel of that old truck thinking I couldn't go on anymore. I was physically and mentally worn out, and I drank that six-pack of beer and fell asleep. I probably slept for four or five hours.

When I woke up, it was dark, and I had a different attitude. I wasn't going to quit! Because I didn't quit, when I walked on stage and got that diploma, there was no one prouder than me—not even the valedictorian I would bet!

I wouldn't have been that proud if I hadn't survived the tremendous scholastic, physical, and financial challenges along the way. I could never have felt that pride if I had not have gone through these tremendous struggles to earn my Associates Degree.

I felt so good and so proud, thinking to myself, "I will never deny my children their right to self-accomplishment and to feel this great pride that I felt that night. The end (of the beginning).

Following this page is an article about Bob Gannon from a publication entitled:

News from the Alumni of Linn Technical College

*FYI: This was written 11 years after Bob graduated from Linn Tech. Yet of all the students who had graduated from Linn Tech, he was the second student they decided to do a story about who attended Linn Tech. The reason they chose Bob as an example was not because of his scholastic ability but because of his determination to refuse to **Never Give Up** as he battled the insurmountable odds to graduate with a degree that would allow him to get a good job. Bob became an inspiration to others.*

Career Profiles

Bob Gannon
Linn Tech Graduation 1972

Bob Gannon:

Portrait in Determination

"**Never Give Up**" is Bob Gannon's
philosophy—a philosophy which has served him
well throughout the years leading to career
success and personal fulfillment. Bob's journey

from student in special education classes to successful electronics technician was not an easy one. It included nine years in the Marine Corps with two hours of duty in Vietnam, a serious war injury, and subsequent long, arduous recovery, and three difficult years at Linn Tech struggling to prepare himself for a changed society,

In 1960, when Bob graduated from high school in Argyle, Missouri, he was not equipped to go to college or to find a job. Because of undiagnosed dyslexia, Bob had been a poor student in special education classes. He felt his best alternative was to enter the service after graduation. The day after he graduated, Bob went to St. Louis to join the Navy. The Navy recruiter happened to be out, and Bob joined the Marine Corps where he served for nine years.

Bob's career in the Marine Infantry was interesting and varied. He spent time in Hawaii and California in the Military Police, and two years in the Phillipines.

Bob received intensive training in reconnaissance and in 1965 had his first tour of duty in Vietnam. He was part of a five-man reconnaissance team whose mission was to locate and map part of the Ho Chi Minh Trail.

After a successful mission, Bob was transferred back to the States where he spent a year in North Carolina in charge of a rifle range and a year in Wilmington, Delaware, in charge of casualty notification.

A second tour of duty in Vietnam culminated in Bob's being seriously wounded. He spent 1-½ years recovering in hospitals from Japan to Memphis. Finally ready for medical duty, Bob was assigned to take charge of the rifle range in Quantico, Virginia, where he taught shooting and ran the pistol range for the shooting team.

During his time in the service, Bob would occasionally think of returning to a small town in mid-Missouri and would ask himself, "What's there for me?" After his discharge from the service, Bob had a chance to find out. He left the Marine Corps with $600 in his pocket and joined his family in Westphalia. Bob did a personal evaluation of himself and decided he could do nothing without training. He used his $600 to buy a 1952 Chevy truck and a chain saw and supported his family by cutting and selling firewood as he investigated educational and training opportunities. He considered attending Lincoln University and then met some students from Linn Tech. The idea of a two-year program interested him, and he decided to visit the college. Bob recalls talking to James Symmonds, who was then Director of Special Services, and Bob Osman, electronics instructor. "They really encouraged me. I had taken only had general math in high school, and I failed the pretest for the electronics program." Nevertheless, with encouragement from Mr. Symmonds and Mr. Osman, and calling upon his philosophy of never giving up, Bob enrolled in the electronics program.

The first year was very difficult for Bob.

"I was really scared, but everything was very personalized. There was always someone there to help me."

Bob received special help from his instructors and worked very hard. His diligence paid off. By his second year, Bob was maintaining a B+ average. His success encouraged him to stay a third year and complete the electronics program in computers.

After graduating from Linn Tech, Bob went to work for Explorer Pipeline as an electrical/mechanical technician.. He traveled around for a year installing individual controls and computers. He began with the maintenance crew tightening nots and bolts for two months and was a welder's helper for four months. He started working for Explorer along with three men from Oklahoma, and by the end of six months, he was the only one of the one of the four to remain and become a technician. Bob attributes this to the self-discipline he learned in the Marines and the fact that he had to work hard to get through Linn Tech.

Over the years, Bob has advanced to the position of senior technician and is involved with all phases of electrical and mechanical work on the pipeline. From 20% to 30% of Bob's work is done on computers. According to Bob, it takes five or six years to become really knowledgeable in this field, and staying knowledgeable requires continual training and updating. "The life of equipment is five years. After that it must be updated. We (technicians) must do research to know what parts are available. The technicians buy most of their own parts and research them.

Bob is constantly reading to keep up with changes. The company sends him to Tulsa twice a year for upgrade training, and he has attended schools in St. Louis and Nebraska.

Bob finds his job very rewarding. "I do something different every day. It's not the same routine. It's very challenging working on very complex, very sophisticated piece of machinery. I love the challenge. Every year I can look back and see how much I have learned."

In discussing his career, Bob points out:

"I probably wouldn't have a career at all if it hadn't been for Linn Tech. I was completely lost. I got a lot of individual attention. My success at Linn Tech built up my confidence."

Bob's interests and hobbies reflect the fact that he hasn't forgotten the help he received along the way to success. A lot of Bob's spare time is devoted to helping others. Bob worked with boxing teams in St. Louis for eight years, and when he moved to St. Peters, he started the St. Peters Track Club (ages 5-18), he organized runs and raised money to send teams to New Jersey and Oklahoma, and to go to the Nationals in

Wisconsin. He is now organizing a run for the Special Olympics. He is trying to start a Special Olympics in St. Peters that is separate from the St. Louis group and now is raising money to buy uniforms and banners.

Bob also coaches a women's softball team. In the five years he has been coaching, the teams have been in first place every year except one.

Bob's children seem to be following in his footsteps. His son, Joseph, is a Marine stationed in Hawaii. His daughter, Patricia, is interested in a technical career and is thinking of attending Linn Tech to study electronics when she graduates next spring.

Bob has helped Explorer Pipeline hire Linn Tech students by conducting campus interviews. He advises young people to select a field with job opportunities. Look at what you're interested in, know the job market, and go after what suits you. Money alone can't make you happy. It can be tough if you don't like what you are doing. Know what you want to do and **Never Give Up**!

Bob at the computer in Explorer Pipeline's Illinois office. The Woodriver Tank Farm. This Daniels computer monitors the operation of four separate pipelines by measuring the expansion and contraction of gasoline due to temperature variations and controlling the amount of gasoline that is pumped to various distributors.

MY MOST UNFORGETTABLE CHARACTER

In the Reader's Digest there were often stories about unforgettable characters. It was during these tough times that I met the most unforgettable character in my life. His name was Norvel Yoker.

I was looking for a place to cut wood, driving up and down different farm roads asking farmers if they had any timber to cut. I needed good timber for cutting cord wood if I was going to make any money. There was no profit in cutting small trees; I needed big ones to fill my truck bed. At the end of a long, gravel road was an old farmhouse, probably 100 years old, with a big old guy sitting on the porch. I went up and asked if he had any wood to cut. He said, "Yeah, I got about 60 acres of it out there." I asked, "Can we take a look at it?" He said, "Well, why don't you sit down for a minute. It's been there for 60 years, and it's probably going to be there a little longer. Sit down and drink a beer with me."

I found out Norvel was a Marine, and he served in the Boxer Rebellion in China. He had pictures of the war, and some of them were pretty gruesome. Norvel had spent his life in Chicago working on concrete floors as a machinist, and he had two bad knees. He was in a lot of pain walking around, but he was a tough man and had a dream. I think he owned 250 acres all totaled. He had a dream to raise cattle on his land. Most of his land was woods and brush. He wanted his land cleared in order to grow more grass for the cattle to be able to graze. So he was glad I was there to start clearing it off. He was the kindest man I ever ran into.

Many times I would get stuck in my old truck, and I would walk over to Norvel's house, and Norvel would get his tractor and pull me out. Whenever I had trouble with my truck, he was always there to help me fix it; and I tried to help him. I was always amazed at his bad legs and how he would be limping around and cutting brush. I would think, "Man, at this rate, he'll never get that land cleared off." A week later, I would be shocked to see how much he had actually gotten done! He didn't have any money to pay for help to put up hay, and he would pull his tractor and trailer in the area of the bales that were laying on the ground in the middle of the field, throw the bales on the trailer, and then he would lean on the wagon for a while resting those bad legs. Then he would move his tractor to another bunch of bales and continue the same pattern. It would be amazing that by the end of the day, he would have all the bales of hay picked up and loaded into his barn.

But he had a lot of bad luck. He had some hogs that were getting ready to go to market, and they got cholera. The whole herd had to be destroyed. The farm was on a hill, and his tractor rolled off the hill when the brakes gave out. The accident broke the front-end wheels off. He still had that big old grin on his face. I asked him, "Norvel, don't you ever get discouraged?" He said, "Well, I'll tell you something young man. I used to get discouraged, but it didn't do me any good." Pretty soon he bought himself another junk tractor and got the other tractor fixed where the front wheels had broken off. It wasn't long until he had two tractors. No matter what happened, no matter how bad or unlucky, he just never got down and never gave up. He always had that big grin on his face, and he overcame everything.

His wife worked, and her sister lived with them. His wife finally talked Norvel into selling the farm because she wanted to move to town. He agreed to sell the farm and move to town to a better house. The old farm house was in bad shape. That was the end of Norvel's dream of having a herd of cows and having his land cleared off, even at his age. He was in his late 70s at this time. It was about a month later that he was in a wheelchair, and it wasn't six months later that he died. His dream was over. I remember meeting his wife, and she was really sad. She told me it was the biggest mistake she ever made in her life—

to move him off that farm. She said the house they bought was really nice, but it meant nothing to her now. She had his body taken back to Chicago where he grew up, and she buried him there. She spent a lot of money putting up a big monument on his grave.

A few years later, after I had graduated from Linn Tech and had a job working on the pipeline, I was traveling through Linn, Missouri. I stopped in one of the local bars for a drink to see if I recognized anyone. There were three or four people there that I knew, and the subject of Norvel Yoker came up. It wasn't long before there were seven or eight people talking about what an inspiration Norvel was to all of us. His good heart and kindness were as indelible as his determination to clear off that land with a couple of bad legs in pursuit of his dream.

In today's world, many people suffer from low self-worth and depression. But God has put a dream in each heart to pursue and accomplish, no matter age or circumstance; each person has a purpose in life. That purpose has nothing to do with materialism, vain success, and selfishness. Rather, the purpose of life is more about goodness and being an example for the Lord. Even though Norvel's dream was raising cattle, it had a spiritual effect on all of us because Norvel was a godly man. We saw his drive and we saw the pain, but we also saw his toughness and willingness to pursue what God had put in his heart.

Who knows just how many lives Norvel affected. He was just an unassuming, desperately poor man living in an old farmhouse. Yet he had influenced all of us in the bar that night, and that proved that it doesn't take money or stature to lead people to Christ or give hope. It just takes a willingness and a toughness to chase the dream that God put in your heart.

MY JOB ON THE PIPELINE

I graduated from Linn Tech with an Associate's degree in electronics, but I didn't get a job. So, I took a third-year course in computer maintenance. It involved a lot of programming (that's when the microchip was just coming out) and the programming was machine language. That was a snap for me. It was the first time in my life I had the thrill of being the best in the class, rather than praying to pass!

In February of 1972, I was in my third year of school. I interviewed with a pipeline company out of Hartford, Illinois and was hired. I quit school and went to work at the pipeline. When school let out in May, Linn Tech sent me a diploma for my associate degree and a report card of all A's.

Five or six years later, Linn Tech started featuring stories in the local newspaper about alumni with outstanding achievements, either while enrolled in school or after graduation. I was the second student (out of thousands of alumni) that was showcased. They talked about my struggles and bringing that old truck to school to use for cutting cord wood. They talked about me having a sixth-grade education and achieving an Associate's degree. When great challenges are met with unstoppable courage, goals are achieved and others are inspired to follow suit.

When I began my job on the newly built pipeline, it was full of water, so they were pressure testing the line. This was to be one of the most modern pipelines in the world, so all the equipment would be first-generation. That meant it would be the first time that the computer systems and all the technology would be tried out. They were expecting lots of trial and error in the initial testing period. As a technician, I would work mostly by myself. I now realized that I could not work for a big company with a lot of people around me. With my PTSD, this job was perfect for me. God had again been looking after my life.

My first day on the job, after a full day's work, the whole crew was sent from Hartford, Illinois to Springfield, Missouri, for some emergency work on the pipeline. They loaded the crew into several trucks and drove us to Springfield, Missouri, to spend the night. I thought there would probably be two or three of us to a room. In those days, Holiday Inns were really the place to stay; they were the quality motels. They put us up in a Holiday Inn and everybody got their own room. We got a great allowance for our meals. We were eating in the best restaurants I had ever eaten in, and we stayed in the best motels. I thought, "Oh, wow, this is really great!"

Sometime later, in February, we were working down on the windy riverfront in Hartford, Illinois in the bitter cold. The windchill factor could reach 20 or 30 degrees below zero! There was a lot of complaining about the cold and some workers even quit. I was thinking, "I don't know why they are complaining or quitting. This is the easiest job I ever had in my life!"

I liked working for this company. Even though my degree was in electronics, we worked on all different types of equipment, not just on computer systems. There was enough variety to keep things from becoming a bore—we worked on pumps, motors, hydraulics and more; we ordered our own parts; we oversaw our own problems. We had a lot of authority over the job we were working on and could hire machinists for machine help. If we had a job in the field and needed engineering help, we called engineering and got their advice. Engineering purchased most of the big, new equipment, but we purchased all the replacement parts.

The pipeline was really a great job, and I loved working alone. Probably at least 80% of the time we set our own schedules. unless we were on a big job. We each had our own area we were responsible for. My area required a lot of traveling and that is probably when my drinking problems began.

The first year really changed my life because I didn't have anything—no furniture, no money. We had nothing. I was making $4.50 an hour, and we worked day and night. Sometimes we just slept on the floor of the stations, and after some rest, we got up and went back to work troubleshooting and getting the line operational. My first check was over $900 after taxes for two weeks' work, and my lifestyle really began to change. I was able to buy a nice car, live in a nice apartment, and eventually, purchase a house. It was the first time in my life I could buy stuff for my family and start living a better life.

We labored at that grueling, time-consuming pace for three years, but I never hated going to work; I loved going to work. I loved solving problems. One of my favorite jobs was major field pump repairs. We had 2000 and 4000 horsepower motors hooked to our pumps on the main pipeline. When they would go down, there could be some major problems. It might require working 15 or 16 hours a day for maybe a week or two. I was on a job watching the sun come up and thinking, "I'm going to be here tonight when the sun goes down." But I loved those challenges because while we were out there in the field, the company gave us complete control of that job. We could hire people, have machine shops on standby, bring parts in; if we needed engineering, we could call for help and get metallurgists, whatever was needed, engineering was right there to back us up and help us with answers to some questions that we didn't have the knowledge to answer. It was a great feeling when we would finally start that pump up and it would run and run smoothly.

When I was going to school, I slept very little because I was so far behind in my classes. The little sleep I did manage to get was interrupted by posttraumatic stress. If I got three hours of sleep a day, I could manage pretty well. Everything sort of culminated when I was hired on at the pipeline. Memories of war never bothered me too much when I was distracted with school work (although there were some spells of flashbacks and crying). But during the years of working on the pipeline, accumulated stress had been pushed aside began to surface.

The first years of working on the pipeline were pretty good because it seemed like we were working day and night. But a few years later, after we got all of the bugs worked out of the equipment, things slowed and we went back to working a normal work schedule—on the road and working an eight-hour day, then, getting to our motel at maybe 5 o'clock in the afternoon. I would often be by myself at 5 o'clock, and I was just antsy. I had to be moving all the time. I couldn't sit down. I couldn't do things like a normal person, like watch television, so I wound up hitting the bars and bringing alcohol back to my room. I would drink about half the night until I could sleep for a while. It never bothered me for work; I would be up the next morning and ready for work, but as time went on, the drinking got worse. It was especially bad when I wasn't on the road and was in town instead, working out of the tank farm in Illinois. As soon as I would get off work, I would get some beer and go home and start drinking.

In the idle time, I would have flashbacks and depression. I would find myself on a lonely road somewhere crying and angry at God over my platoon that was ambushed and killed.

When I wasn't working on the pipeline, I threw myself into my kids' lives. My daughter ran track. My son was an amateur fighter. When we moved to St. Peters, there was no track program, and my daughter wanted to run, so I started the St. Peters Track Club. It was just for kids and high school students, and we found two really good coaches—one for track and field, and the other for cross-country. They were really great at what they did.

Then, I started up the St. Charles County Striders which was a club of grownups, and we put on marathons, half-marathons and

10-K runs. Half of all the money we made was put into the St. Peters Track Club and helped the kids when they went to track meets and to nationals; it would pay most of their way.

Bob's two children in
their teenage years:
Trish and Joe

We did fundraisers by putting on races. One such fundraiser helped a school for children with special needs go to the Special Olympics. We raised $1000, which was more than enough to pay for the uniforms they needed! I was getting all kinds of accolades, even getting written up in the local paper. I also coached Little League softball and women's softball.

I was founder and president of the Debug Computer Club. WordPerfect and other computer programs had just come out, and many people needed instruction on how to utilize them. We put on free monthly classes and became the second largest computer club in St. Louis in a one year's time. The only club that had more members than us was McDonald-Douglas, which is a company that builds military airplanes (now called Boeing).

I did all this to stay busy as I continued to work for 33 years on the pipeline. I think my heart was in the right spot, but my drinking got worse.

Drinking and time alone on the road led to two divorces. As time went on, the torment intensified, and the flashbacks got worse. I tried everything to numb the pain—I went to bars, picked up women, and became unfaithful. We are made in the image of Christ, it's not possible to live a sinful life and have peace at the same time. So, there was turmoil. I sank so low, I didn't even want to look in the mirror anymore.

I was working in south St. Louis, severely depressed and in a really bad marriage. I pulled up to a stop sign, and everything hit me—my life, everything I had done, the divorces, the sinful life I led. I just began crying. I finally hit bottom. It was one of the first times in my life I just totally broke down sobbing. Something tapped me on the shoulder, and a voice in my truck said, "It's almost over." The voice was very loud. I remember thinking, "How could God love me after the life I have led for the past 20 years and after I have cursed his name many times?" I could feel God's sympathy and pity for my pain.

Romans 5:8: *God proved his love for us in that while we were still sinners, Christ died for us.*

The very next day, my life began to change, and I started picking myself up. God began moving obstacles that had been holding me back, and I then began to experience a gradual and daily spiritual growth.

BIKING/JUDY ENTERS MY LIFE

As my faith began to burgeon, the urge to drink was greatly diminished. I tried church, but the horrors I had seen on the battlefield continued to their toll. It was absolutely imperative for me to keep myself distracted from those memories, and I continued to throw myself into many different things.

I purchased a cross-country bicycle, and to keep myself busy, I did a lot of cycling. I rode that bicycle 3000 to 4000 miles a year. I took several bicycle trips. The first trip I took was riding from St. Louis to Nashville. Then, a year or so later, I took a 1000-mile trip where I rode from St. Louis to St. Paul, Minnesota, up the river road which followed the Mississippi River. It was a beautiful ride. I tried to do 100 miles a day while on trips. I never was in a hurry. I got up at 6 o'clock in the morning, and I would stop in all the little towns. It was interesting! People were eager to talk when they saw a stranger peddling into town and were curious about where I had come from. A lot of times I camped out, and people would invite me over to eat with them. It was great.

While I was training for my third bicycle trip to South Dakota, somebody gave me a flyer to a 25-mile ride that was being organized. Most of my rides were either 50, 75 or 100 miles, so I decided I would get there early, go out and ride 50 miles and come back. I went out, rode 50 or 60 miles and came back while it was still early. No cyclists had shown up yet, but I saw that they were setting up their registration tent, so I thought, "Well, I'll just go over there and shoot the bull since I have nothing else to do."

I met a girl named Judy, and we hit it off right away. There was an ice cream stand nearby, and I said, "Hey, after I come back from the ride, do you want to get an ice cream?" She said that would be great, and that started our relationship. She was also into biking, so we started biking together. We cycled on the Katy Trail doing 70- to 90-mile rides.

I was still training for my third, long distance bicycle trip, almost ready to leave. Riding 100 miles without extra weight was much easier than riding with a 45 pound backpack. The pack created a lot of wind resistance, so I needed to practice with it to prepare for my trip. I was pushing pretty hard, coming down through West Alton Bottoms, and I ripped a muscle in the back of my calf. I mean it RIPPED; you could actually feel the tear in the muscles. I had to go to a chiropractor for six months before I could start training again and my trip was on hold for a year.

In the meantime, I married Judy! She was a Christian, and she made sure we went to church on Sundays. I began letting God be a part of my life.

In December, I started training again on a stationary bike and I prepared for the trip that had been delayed. I started training early in hopes to leave early in June while it was still cool. I knew that in July and August, the blacktop roads would be sizzling hot, and now in my 50's, I had the sense to avoid a heat stroke!

Judy was really proud of me during training. She would tell her friends I was going to ride to South Dakota. The channel 4 weatherman in St. Louis gave me updates on a regular basis. The first of June, a couple weeks before my planned departure, I called in to ask him about the forecast. I was hoping to avoid the rain that had been so prevalent that spring. The weatherman said, "Hey, it looks like you've got a good shot for the next seven days."

I went home and told Judy, "I'm leaving in the morning. I'm packing my bike up tonight; I've got a seven-day break in the weather." She went into hysteria and asked me, "Are you really going to do this?" I said, "Yeah, I'm going to do it. You watched me train for it." She tried to talk me out of it. All of the sudden, she became very worried.

In the morning, I got up and headed out. I went down through West Alton, Missouri, where I could catch a ferry that took me across the Mississippi River into Illinois. I was probably about 15 miles into Illinois and got into a monstrous shower; it just POURED down, so I was soaking wet! But I rode all the way into South Dakota and caught a train home. That was my last bike trip, but I always loved it. I'm 78 now, and I think maybe I could do one more; I don't know.

CELEBRATE RECOVERY

When I was first transferred to Springfield (Mt. Vernon), a friend of mine asked me to help him with a jail ministry, and God used this to help lure me back into the church. For three years, I went with him, and we took the ministry into the large county jail in Mt. Vernon, Missouri. I wasn't convinced that we were helping very many people or changing their lives. We were bringing the gospel, but when the guys would get out of jail, and they would go right back into the same environment from whence they came. Many of them would be back in jail again in a short period of time and maybe on their way to prison again. So I never really felt like I was accomplishing much in the jail ministry.

Then I was contacted by some people who were starting the Celebrate Recovery program at Ridgecrest Baptist Church in Springfield, Missouri. They asked me if I would like to help them start the program. I said, "Sure, but I really don't have any problems." Can you imagine me saying, "I really don't have any problems" after growing up in an alcoholic and abusive home, having a learning disability, serving two tours in Vietnam, 20 years of alcoholism, and two divorces?! I was amazed to find out how dysfunctional I really was and how many people I had hurt from all of my above problems. I got involved with that ministry and went through the training. When they started the CR program, I became the small group chemical dependency leader. It was at this point I realized I began my own healing through the lessons, the testimonies, the small group meetings, and the Celebrate Recovery step study.

Later in my life, after I retired from my pipeline job, what happened to me in Vietnam haunted me every day. I finally got into a program at the VA to deal with the ongoing effects of trauma devastating my life. The program was called long-term exposure treatment. The psychiatrist didn't expect me to complete the program because of the devastating emotional breakdowns I had when dealing with the issues I experienced in Vietnam. When I did complete it, she offered grim odds about whether or not I'd go on to attempt suicide when I first started the program.

I give Celebrate Recovery the credit for my completion of the VA program because I learned in Celebrate Recovery that the only way to get well is to attack an issue head-on. I'm still serving as a Celebrate Recovery leader 18 years later, and I am still growing as I help others do the same. Little did I know that I really did have my own problems and lots of them! **Silly me!**

I still wanted to do a prison ministry. I was working with Les Palmer, one of the people who started CR at Ridgecrest Baptist Church, so the church sent Les and me to a seminar in Kentucky on prison ministries. Shortly after we came back, I started Celebrate Recovery Inside at the Ozark Correctional Facility in Fordland, Missouri. I had been doing this program for four months, and I could see that it was struggling. It was poorly attended, and I began to realize that I didn't understand the prison system or what the inmates were going through.

In Celebrate Recovery, there are different levels of leadership. I began to train the inmates to run the program. It took me about two months of going in on Saturdays and other times to meet with them. I took CR training materials so they would have reference manuals, and the inmates who were trained could now train other inmates to become leaders. When I turned it over to them, things changed. We started a step study. A step study is an in-depth course that lays the soul bare through unflinching honesty. The level of sharing and sincerity it requires evaporates guilt! We started with about 16 men in a step study on Saturday and Sunday nights, and within two months, we had 140 to 160 men in attendance.

On Friday nights, we had the prison band play. Afterward, we would break down into small groups of 6 to 8 men to share our hurts, habits and hangups. People who had completed the step study shared their personal testimonies of how it had changed their lives and thinking. They shared how their faith had grown and how they were now relying on God to guide their lives.

The leaders in the step study began to organize different events to promote Celebrate Recovery. They would meet the busses of new inmates who were coming to the prison. They organized CR softball tournaments. I was amazed. They planned many events I thought would fail, but it always worked and even became a model program for all of the CR programs throughout the United States. It changed the whole atmosphere of the prison. They used to have lots of problems with the inmates—the whole prison would be locked down at times. But that all changed as CR attendance began to swell!

There were four different books in Celebrate Recovery dealing with different issues of one's life. I realized that most men in prison have never gotten an award, and this was a really, really tough program to get through, so we began to celebrate their achievements. This was so effective! New groups were starting all the time, so men were staggered in reaching their important milestones. I saw the men transforming before my very eyes as they worked through the books. I could almost tell what phase of the program they were in just by observing their hope and confidence arise.

Celebrate Recovery leaders would meet the busses of incoming inmates to tell them the benefits of CR. Many times I heard stories like, "Man, I got off the bus and there was old George. George and I spent time in this prison and that prison, and when I got off the bus and looked into his eyes, I said, 'George, what has happened to you? You're not the same person. I see peace.'" Peace seemed to be the common thing each inmate was searching for. Many of them joined Celebrate Recovery because they wanted the peace that they had seen in the men who were in the step study program.

I wanted to give each man an award after they completed each one of the four books. I think the first award was a Bible, and the second award was a CR coin. The fourth book award would be a CR completion coin.

We couldn't figure out something for the third award, so I told the secretary of the church to just order something, and she ordered some little blue bracelets. Well, I wasn't in tune to prison regulations and didn't bother to check out to see whether the bracelets would violate the prison dress code, so the people who received the first CR bracelets got into major trouble for wearing the bracelets. I now realized I had violated the prison uniform code.

The next week when I came in, I got chewed out by the sergeant of the guard, the lieutenant of the guard, and many others. Many of the men who had the bracelets on were thrown in the hole for wearing the bracelets, and it turned out to be a mess. But the men loved their bracelets. They loved them because they said to me, "Bob, when we're out in the yard, we can recognize our brothers in CR, and it's a comfort. We are going to form prayer groups, and we are going to pray that the warden will change the dress code to allow for the CR bracelets. Bob, you write a letter to the warden and ask him to change and let these bracelets be part of the uniform prison code." I knew that the warden wasn't going to change the prison code. I talked to some of the guards. Some of them had been guards in prisons for 30 years, and they told me, "Bob, there's no way that they are going to change the uniform prison code for a Christian program." But I couldn't talk the prisoners out of it, so I wrote the letter to the warden, and they formed a prayer group and were praying for these bracelets.

It was a Friday afternoon when I was heading out to the prison for the Friday night program, and I was thinking, "How am I going to tell them that the warden turned them down, and how am I going to take the negative away from it and make it somewhat positive because I know that when this happens, a lot of them are going to lose their faith in God?" I was worried because I knew that this could damage the program pretty heavily. I got a call from the warden's office, and I remember thinking, "Oh, crap!" It was the secretary, and she said, "Bob, the warden has approved those bracelets as a new uniform code for the prison." I was sitting there thinking, "And I'm taking the gospel to these people??!"

FARMING IN MT. VERNON

In 1995, I had a chance to transfer from the tank farm at Woodriver to Mt. Vernon, Missouri. I always wanted to move to the country. I grew up in the country. My responsibility in Mt. Vernon was to take care of two remote pipeline booster stations. One station was in Mt. Vernon, and the other station was in Vinita, Oklahoma.

Mt. Vernon was just 24 miles west of Springfield, so Judy and I bought a farm and two horses for Judy and me. We joined some riding clubs. We purchased a stud horse, raised horses and sold them. The stud horse we purchased was a beautiful black and white, double-registered Tennessee Walker/Spotted Saddle horse. We also bred horses for other people. We put out a bunch of flyers advertising our stud horse for breeding. It was unbelievable...within a week we had 14 mares to breed! We really didn't know much about breeding and were quite unprepared. We just started breeding everything we could, and within a short time, we became very efficient at breeding. Judy wasn't scared of trying anything new. She was always there helping me, whether it was breeding mares or, later, working cattle.

Raising horses and cattle kept me busy, but the accumulated stress of wartime memories crept in even deeper. I would take my truck out to check on the cows, have a flashback, and just cry my heart out. When I eventually retired from the pipeline, the flashbacks and nightmares got worse, and now I had a lot of time on my hands! My life was totally collapsing. I had completely isolated myself from Judy. I didn't want to be around anybody. Phone calls to my children became almost nonexistent—I would call them maybe once a year. Even when my part-time work for the pipeline took me to the towns where my children lived, I did not visit them. I built a wall around myself and wasn't about to let anyone in.

Judy was always interested in music, so she began staying busy with music lessons and learning how to play the guitar. She joined some local jams in the Springfield area where people just sat around and played music together. Every night there was a gathering of musicians, so she had lots of opportunities to play the guitar. She became pretty good! Next, she bought a mandolin and fell in love with playing it. She was also a top-notch singer and joined some bands. She would always go perform in the nursing homes to brighten up the residents' lives. She had a spirituality about her, and she always made sure we went to church.

I encouraged Judy in her musical aspirations, so she continued playing with bands in nursing homes and shows. Her next pursuit was the fiddle—she bought one and began to play. She became a pretty decent fiddle player! Judy really worked hard at everything she pursued. She would practice that fiddle at 1 or 2 o'clock in the morning, as well as the mandolin and guitar, until she became pretty proficient at them all.

This was convenient for me because I was trying to isolate myself. Having just retired from the pipeline, post-traumatic stress was kicking into overdrive and things were spiraling out of hand. I was having spells. I was going off on myself. I was crying. A lot of times I just wanted to be alone.

Judy endured some really difficult times with me, and she never complained. She knew what I was going through, and she would try to help me. She stuck with me. There were times I was so depressed that I didn't want to talk or communicate at all. I just would go off by myself and spend a whole day in isolation. Judy was intuitive and just seemed to understand that I needed space. If I wasn't at the house, she would go out to make music with her band. She had wisely developed an outlet for herself to keep from falling into the pits of depression. I know it bothered her that she could not help ease my PTSD, but she always treated me well.

The families of combat survivors suffer immensely because of the breakdown that arises when their veteran is unable to communicate a pain that they cannot understand or describe.

MOVING TO ROLLA, MISSOURI

After spending 21 years on our Mt. Vernon farm, we decided to move to be closer to family, so we moved to Rolla. We bought just 20 acres and sold our cattle.

When we moved to Rolla, Judy started her own ministry going into the Alzheimer's ward at the Veterans Home. Men were locked in that ward and couldn't get out, and she would put a show on for them. She went over there once a week. She would sing for an hour and a half. She would come home, and her voice would totally be gone. She would tell me stories about how some men hadn't spoken in years, but they would just break out in song. She gave it all she had. She had a real heart for people and her faith. We always went to church. Praying her rosary on a daily basis was very important to her.

GOODBYE DEAREST JUDY

Judy continued her music ministries, and she was still going to jams. Then Judy digressed from being a very independent and self-sufficient person to being afraid to be alone. She became very depressed and then became very sick. She had always been a daredevil! She loved the roller coaster rides or anything like that. One of the last trips we had canoeing together was down the Current River in Missouri, and there was a bluff, probably 60 to 80 feet high. There were kids jumping off the bluff into the water. Now Judy was 68 years old, and she said, "I'm going to jump off that bluff. I tried to discourage her, but that's who she was, and I've got one picture of her climbing that bluff, and she jumped off. Afterward, she said, "You know what? That was fun! I've got to do it again!" She jumped off that bluff into the Current River twice, and it wasn't long after that when her illness really got serious. In the spring of 2020, she passed away.

I gave a eulogy at her funeral. These were my thoughts: "When we are gone, the impact of our lives is reflected in what people have to say about us. They're not going to talk about the houses owned or the cars driven, the careers, or the big-shot successes—they're going to talk about the heart. They're going to talk about the good things that will be remembered."

I am so proud of Judy's life and all the years she dedicated going to nursing homes and playing her music and going to Victory Mission with me in Springfield for 13 years. She would go into the missions and sing and play her instruments for the homeless. She supported me.

I'll always be sorry that Judy is gone. We had a great life and lots of fun. I'm proud of the way she conducted herself and the way she served God.

I have a picture of Judy on her horse, Jackpot, who she raised from a colt. Judy and Jackpot rode all over together. I still own Jackpot. He is 20 some years old now, and I'll keep him until he passes on. That was Judy's horse, and she really loved her horse.

THE EFFECTS OF
POSTTRAUMATIC STRESS DISORDER

The Veterans Administration strongly recommended a program for me that was called Long-Term Exposure Treatment, and it was to deal with the worst trauma that I suffered in Vietnam which was the artillery rounds falling short and killing so many women and children as the story was told within this book and titled "The Village of Nightmares". The crux of the program was to spend a whole hour repeating the same story over and over in an effort to desensitize the trauma. Then she (the psychiatrist) would tape the story, and I would have to go home and listen to it every day. When I went the first time, she asked me to tell the story of the village that I inadvertently destroyed, but I couldn't tell it. All I could do was cry. I just emotionally totally broke down. I was crying so hard, I couldn't stop the tears. But this is how the long-term program works. After a time, I gathered myself together and was able to tell the story about the village and killing the people.

They never give you advice on how you should think or what they think you should think. When I finally got my story told, she would say, "Okay, what did the Viet Cong do after the artillery rounds fell short and hit the village?" I said, "Well, they left. They knew they were found out." She said, "Oh, so what do you think would have happened if they wouldn't have left? If those artillery rounds wouldn't have hit the village?" I said, "A battalion of Marines probably would have been sent in to battle the Viet Cong." Then she asked, "How many of the Marines do you think would have gotten killed, and what about the firefight between the Marines and the Viet Cong? How many people in the village do you think would have gotten killed?"

So she always gave you different scenarios to change the way that you thought that possibly, if the Marines would have come in, how many Marines would have been killed, and maybe the village would have suffered a worse consequence.

She also gave me challenges to visit my children. These were challenges that she gave me directly and was pretty adamant that I do them. This was how bad the wall was that I had built between myself and my children. One of the challenges she gave me was to visit my daughter. I was working for the pipeline part-time, and I was going to be staying in Rolla, Missouri. She said, "When you stay in Rolla, I want you to visit your daughter in Jefferson City." I said, "Okay."

I got to the motel in Rolla, and I called my daughter and said, "Hey, I'll meet you guys at this certain restaurant, and I'll buy you supper." My daughter said, "No, Dad, I'm going to cook supper. I want you to come to the house."

I'll tell you, my heart dropped to my stomach. I automatically was thinking, "I can't do that. I can't go there." But I've always been one if you give me a challenge,

I would do it. I drove to her house, and all the time in my mind I was thinking, "Call her and tell her you can't make it. Give her some excuse. Turn around." The urge to turn that vehicle around and go back to the motel was just overwhelming, but I didn't, and by the time I hit Jefferson City, I was so nervous that the water was running out of my hands. It was then that I finally realized how bad the posttraumatic stress symptoms had overtaken me.

One of the parts that I was supposed to do was to tell my story. My family knew nothing of what I endured in Vietnam in either tour, and the challenge was to tell some of the things, you know, not gory things. But I got there, and I sat out front for a minute. I just wanted to leave, but I didn't. I got myself together and walked up to the door. Once I was there for 15 or 20 minutes, I pretty much relaxed. After we ate, we all retired to the patio, and I shared some of the very emotional stories for the first time ever. We all shed tears as I related these happenings, but they now understood some of the trauma I suffered in Vietnam and why I acted in the manner I did through all those years.

I could see the great effect that it had on my family. That was the beginning of the healing of the relationship with my children. She challenged me to do the same thing with my son. So I repeated the same process. It was uncomfortable for a long time. It was something I had to really force myself to do. But today I see the great rewards I have from getting to really know my son and respect him as the man he has grown into.

Many veterans' families have told me how their son or daughter they sent off to war was not the same person who came back from war. They oftentimes eventually walked out and left. I knew of one veteran who left his mother. The mother and her veteran son were really close before he left for war, but when he came back from war, he soon left home and he didn't communicate with his mother anymore; or you hear children talk about the same thing—how their veteran father or mother is emotionally cold and seldom hugs or tells them they love them. So that's the wall that is built, and it takes a lot of effort and a lot of years to slowly tear that wall down. The wall wasn't built all at once; it was built brick by brick at a time, and the only way we can take it down is brick by brick at a time.

It has probably taken me about 15 years to disassemble my wall, and now I have a normal relationship with my children. I am beginning to feel emotions that I never had before, and I give thanks to the VA in Mt. Vernon and the psychiatrist who really pushed me. I am very thankful for today, and I tell veterans they need to get into treatment.

Once you were a warrior for your country, and you battled some great odds. You were willing to risk your life and die. Now I'm asking you to be a warrior for your family and do the same for your family;

don't quit the program, stick it out. I tell you this because I remember sitting in a veterans' group one time, and I was on my third marriage, and out of everyone in that group, I was the one who had been married the fewest times. That's why I'm telling you, "GET IN TREATMENT, STICK IT OUT AND **NEVER GIVE UP!**"

THE VETERANS ADMINISTRATION IS DIFFERENT NOW!

A friend talked me into going to the Vietnam Veterans of America to file my claim. While I was there, the man who was filling out my claim form kept looking at me, and he finally said, "You've got a severe case of posttraumatic stress. I became very angry at him, and I thought he must be an idiot because I was a Recon Marine. I went through some really, really tough Recon training. Recon Marines don't have posttraumatic stress. He then began to read the symptoms, and then it hit me really hard, and all I could do was just start crying. I knew I had a very serious case of posttraumatic stress. He told me, "You need to get into treatment." I said, "I'll never go back to the VA ever because of my earlier experience in 1972 where they called me a fake and a fraud!" He said, "Bob, it's changed. It's really changed." He told me of a VA office right across town that dealt with posttraumatic stress issues. He said, "Let me call the VA and see if I can get you in." He knew if I went home, I would never come back. So he called them, and they said they would make room for me. He talked me into going over there, and it was all changed. It was amazing!

For the next six months I was seeing a psychiatrist three days a week. I went through two different sessions of long-term exposure treatment. It was at the VA Hospital there in Mt. Vernon, and the psychiatrists there were just great. It was just unbelievable how they changed my life. After I had completed the program, they told me I was in such bad shape when I went into the program, they only gave me a 50/50 chance of not committing suicide. All of the psychiatrists were women with the exception of one or two men. Their schedules were full, but they were so dedicated to serving us, they said if we had a problem and needed to see them, even if we didn't have an appointment, they would give up their lunch hour.

The VA has changed for the good, and I say this because I know there are a lot of Vietnam veterans that had the same experience I did when I got out. They were intimidated by the VA. They too were called names like "fake" and "fraud." Some of the people in the VA said we didn't fight a real war. My experience in 1972 was when the Marine Corps removed me from the temporarily retired list into 50% permanent disability and gave me a medical discharge because of my injuries. They told me to go to the VA and file a claim. I scheduled an appointment at the VA Hospital in Jefferson Barracks, St. Louis, Missouri, and I got examined for my injuries by a doctor. She examined me and then said, "You are nothing but a fake and a fraud. There is nothing wrong with. I am going to recommend no disability." I was devastated. I felt my country had turned against me. I caused a lot of my own injuries because I would **never give up**; I had many multiple sprains which caused both legs to have stretched ligaments as well as lots of swelling and pain, but I hid my injuries so I could continue my job as a platoon sergeant. I knew I was needed. However, there came a day when I sprained my left ankle so bad it swelled up so much that I couldn't even get my boot on. I was so hurt when I walked out of the VA that day, I felt I would never go back and face that humiliation again. I only tell this story because I know there are a lot of Vietnam veterans who have faced the same humiliation as I did that day, and that is why they mistrust the VA still today.

I also want to encourage you, if you are a veteran or the family of a Vietnam veteran or any veteran, get to the VA. The VA today has really changed, and I think, in many cases, today you will get better medical treatment at the VA than on the civilian side. Quite recently I had cataracts removed and stents put in my eyes for glaucoma. Every time I go to the VA Hospital in Columbia, Missouri, someone always greets me and thanks me for my service. All of my medical treatment has been stupendous in this new change of the VA and how veterans are treated today.

I wanted to particularly give kudos to my medical doctor at the Mt. Vernon VA Hospital at this time. My physical condition was so bad that I was having severe blood pressure and heart problems, and she scheduled me to come in every three months rather than the norm of once a year for checkups and multiple tests. I received every heart test known to man, even going to several different hospitals in Arkansas for specialty tests. In all my appointments, she would spend extra time talking to me. She would talk about my mental condition and figure out how she could help me more by adjusting my medications or working closely with my psychiatrists to help me through this time.

BEGIN THE MIRACLE

After 33 years of service, I retired from my pipeline job in 2005. Without the distractions of the job to keep my mind occupied, what happened in Vietnam haunted me every day.

To recap some of my problems caused by posttraumatic stress thus far: In 2008, I was diagnosed by the Veterans Administration with PTSD. They said I was suffering from multiple traumas caused by two tours in Vietnam. My posttraumatic stress and mental state were so severe, I could not remember much about my second tour in Vietnam; my memory had been pretty well wiped out. I could not remember the year I was there or the battalion or the company I was in. All I knew was that I was platoon sergeant of the third platoon. I have been seeing psychiatrists at the Veterans Administration since 2008, and the treatment greatly helped me to deal with the many traumas in the battle and with the demons that were always in my head at that time.

The VA psychiatrist, a great lady, challenged me to restore relationships with my family, among other things. I saw her two times a week and another psychiatrist once a week over a period of several months.

GOD, WHERE ARE YOU?

I didn't have much of a prayer life at this point because the war had caused me to believe that God didn't care about any of us. It seemed that he wasn't hearing us anymore. Maybe random chance or mental toughness determined our lot in life? After I was injured during my second tour, I was sent to the naval hospital in Memphis, Tennessee, where I found out my platoon had been ambushed (most were killed) two days after I was medivacked off the battlefield. I became so angry at God on that day, I swore I would go to hell before I would ever kneel or bow to a God who had not allowed me to be with my men when they were ambushed. I was the platoon sergeant. The men counted on me. I felt I let them down. I still today feel the guilt of not being there and letting them down.

The night I was injured, they couldn't medivac me out until the next morning. Some of the men in the platoon just kept asking me, "Do you think you're going to make it back? Who is going to take over the platoon? There is no one left with any experience as a platoon sergeant."

I tried to calm them down by saying that everything would be alright, but I knew in my heart there was no one left with any experience. The next morning when they loaded me on the medivac helicopter, I was thinking, "I'm going to live. I'm going to see my children." Little did I know those words were going to haunt me for the rest of my life because it's a platoon sergeant's job to tend to his men's welfare before his own. So even today, I still feel selfish because I should have been thinking about their families, not just my own.

I blamed God for my injuries, and for the next 20 years I lived on the dark side of alcohol, anger, and a very sinful life. I asked God many times through all my traumas, "Why do you keep me here? Why didn't you let me die with my men?"

It was years later, and I was still suffering from depression and guilt over what happened to the platoon. I asked God again why he had not allowed me to be with my platoon when they were ambushed. That night I had a dream that I died, and all the men who were killed in the ambush were there to welcome me. They had forgiven me when I could not forgive myself. They were all smiling and appeared to be surrounded by serenity and joy. They were above me, and they had their arms reaching down as if to pull me up to where they were, and I knew they were all in heaven. I know God allowed this dream because he felt my pain, anger, and guilt. But I needed to go through this pain, anger and guilt so I could work with veterans today who struggle with these same type of issues.

Has God taken all the pain and struggle from my past? No, he has not. I still struggle with my past life and some of the people I hurt during my alcoholic years. I still struggle with a serious case of posttraumatic stress disorder. But it is in these struggles that I am reminded of those poor souls who are struggling with many types of addictions. My goal is not for the material things of this world anymore but serving God where I am needed. You see, I'm 78 now in 2020, and I know my time is limited. My goal is that when I stand before God to be judged, he will say, "You **DID** become the masterpiece I created you to be!"

It is through the struggles that I still have today that I feel the hurt and the sympathy for those who are struggling too, and that is why I serve. When people say, "Don't you wish God would have taken all of your struggles away?" I say, "No, I'm glad he didn't, because if he took all my struggles away, I wouldn't have the sympathy or the compassion to serve the drug addict, the alcoholic, and the homeless. Because of my struggles, I understand what it's like to be hopeless, I understand what it's like to be raised in a dysfunctional family. Because of what I have experienced in life, I know what it's like to think that God doesn't love me and to wonder why would he allow painful things to happen to me?

GET THEE BEHIND ME SATAN, I NOW HAVE A ROSARY

I grew up in a Catholic church, but about 40 years ago, I pretty much quit going to church. In 2014, my wife and I started attending the Catholic church at St. Ann Seton in Springfield, Missouri. I bought myself a rosary, and I began praying the rosary every day. It was still hard for me to pray because I still had a lot of anger at God because of what happened in Vietnam. And even though I had been bringing the gospel to prisons and jails in a Christian program called Celebrate Recovery for some time, I was still struggling to pray and still struggling with a serious case of posttraumatic stress. I was not trusting God to bring his forgiveness and healing into my own life; I was bringing the gospel to everyone but me.

When I started praying the rosary in hopes of finding some spirituality, Satan would remind me of all the alcoholic, sinful years I'd lived and all of the people I've hurt. But over time, praying the rosary nearly every day, I noticed my anger at God slowly began to diminish, and Satan's influence over me while I was praying the rosary began to fade. However, what happened to the village and the Vietnam people still haunted me daily causing nightmares, flashbacks, and weeks of depression.

MEMORIES STILL BRING FLASHBACKS

Even though I retired from my full-time work on the pipeline in 2005, I was sometimes commissioned on a part-time basis after that. I was working in Texas in May of 2015 and had a major setback. I went into a store for some supplies. As I stood in the checkout line, a small child started crying and then screaming—a sound that always caused flashbacks to what happened the night the rounds were accidentally dropped on the unsuspecting village in Vietnam. By the time I got out of the store, I was in tears reliving that horrific memory.

I was listening to the radio in my truck when I learned a man had fallen off a water tower and was killed. For the next three days, I didn't sleep because of continuous nightmares. I had the nagging thought that if I could climb a water tower ladder and let go, it would all be over. My stress level was so high that I began having out-of-body experiences playing it all out in my mind. As I imagined such a fall, I could actually feel myself floating through the air, free of all the guilt, pain, and grief. I contemplated what it might be like with no more nightmares, no more daytime flashbacks, no more hearing the screaming and the dying of the wounded villagers. Never again would I have to listen to the long wail by that Vietnamese woman and wonder what happened in her family.

A VISION OF A LITTLE GIRL

I was in a horrendous battle with Satan for my life and soul during those three days. I felt so alone and I thought the only one who truly understood what I was going through was a little girl who kept appearing in my recurring dreams. I felt I needed to see the little girl, and I remember saying, "Little girl, little girl, I need to see you. I am so alone, and you are the only one who knows what I am going through."

God put a vision of that little girl's face inside my eyelids. I would shut my eyes, and her picture would be there. The vision calmed me and comforted me. I didn't feel alone anymore. It helped me get through the many emotional breakdowns and the temptations to end my life. The vision was only temporary, however, and after three days, when the worst of the temptations to take my life abated, the vision of the little girl disappeared and has never appeared again.

ENTER ST. THERESE

When I got home from working onsite in Texas, I was very depressed. The little girl's vision had disappeared, and I again felt very alone. I told no one what I was going through. It's really hard for a veteran to relate his experiences which occurred on the battlefield. It's just emotionally hard to talk to others about what we are going through.

The next day, my wife Judy and I attended church, and I picked up a pamphlet on St. Therese, child of Jesus, and she said in the pamphlet, "My mission is to make people love God as I love him, and I will begin after my death to spend my time in heaven doing good on earth. I will let fall a shower of roses." Countless lives have been touched by her intercession. I started praying a daily novena[14] to St. Therese for help. Saints cannot perform miracles, but as Catholics, we ask them to intercede for us and take our needs to Jesus. I chose the route of a saint in desperation because of the anger I still had with God over what happened on the battlefield. I had trouble praying to God because every time I tried to pray directly to him, I would become very angry, and I suppose I felt going through a saint would be a more indirect approach and therefore allow the saint to be my representative to ask God to perform a miracle of relief and restore my belief.

I was on my fifth daily novena when my wife Judy and I took our horses to one of our favorite places to ride—Caney Mountain. It's a beautiful place down around Big Flat, Arkansas, near the Buffalo River, 8 miles down a gravel road, full of nature, spirituality, friendship, and peacefulness.

---

[14] *A novena is a specific prayer for nine days.*

The people who ran it and those who lived there made it extra special. They took us out riding, cooked for us, and gave us the royal treatment. We arrived as guests, but soon felt like family. The whole mountaintop felt like a godly place, and that's why I believe God chose this setting for the miracle to take place.

JUDY & BOB AT CANEY MOUNTAIN

On the evening of the third day, several of us were sitting on the front porch; some were playing music, when a couple came to the horse camp from Central Illinois. Their names were Rob and Karen, and they came with a little girl. Her name was Addie. I was in total disbelief because Addie was the little girl I had seen in my dreams for the past 50 years. I had begun seeing her over 40 years before she was born!

I could not believe what was happening. I had seen her in my dreams, but I never knew she was real. She was the same size, the same build, and her hair was even combed the same way. What was most interesting is that they didn't get to the camp until late at night, and my wife and I were about to leave. They came from Peoria, Illinois, a 600-mile trip to the camp. On the way down, they had a flat tire on their trailer which took a while to repair, then a windstorm came up before they got there, and three trees were blown down across the gravel road leading to the camp. They called for help, and it took chain saws to clear the road so they could get in. I always have believed Satan was trying to stop this testimony because it was about 9:30 at night before they got to the camp and we might have missed them! We could have easily gone back to our room, and this miracle would never have happened. I never told anyone that night what happened; I was having a hard time believing it myself.

The next morning we went riding with Addie's mom Karen. I found out Addie had a disease called tuberous sclerosis which caused tumors on her brain and resulted in seizures. Addie is a special needs child. I felt the need to hold Addie, but I was not sure how this could take place.

When we got back from riding and were getting ready to leave, my wife was paying our bill, and she got in a very long discussion with the lady to whom she was paying the bill. I was sitting on the porch at this time, and Addie and her mom came up and sat down right next to me. It took all the courage I could muster to tell her the story of the village and seeing Addie in my dreams and wondering if she would believe me or think I was some kind of nut, but she just handed me the little girl. As Addie lay her head on my chest, I could feel the outline of her body getting warm, and I knew a miracle was happening at this time. I remember thinking that God had sent a broken little girl to heal this broken veteran.

That was on May 29, 2015, and on that day my nightmares ended, and the flashbacks and sounds of what happened to the village have been emotionally disarmed. Addie's health has greatly improved, and shortly after the miracle, Addie was put on new medications, and her tumor has been dormant since 2015. I was talking to a priest because this little girl's picture had a huge calming effect on me. I was asking him how could this little girl, a special needs girl, have such an effect, and he said, "Because she is special; she is without sin, she is pure, and God can use her." So the next time you see a special needs child, know he or she is pure and is going to heaven.

About a month after the miracle, I asked Addie's mom if she could send me some pictures of her, and she told me she had taken some pictures of Addie, and a cross appeared in one of the pictures. In one of the pictures there was a sand beach that appeared as a gold beach with a cross in the water in the picture. I had found myself doubting if this miracle really took place; *why would God create a miracle for somebody like me?* I had begun to doubt, so God began to reinforce it. About three weeks later they were trail riding, and they took some more pictures. There was a tree cross, and if you blow the picture up, there are some white apparitions that appear to float above the ground quite a ways. They look a bit like the shapes of angels.

It was the last week in November, and I had invited some friends over, Steve and Susan, for supper. That morning after I had finished my novena to St. Therese, praying for Addie, I remembered St. Therese's promise of a shower of roses, and I asked her, "Are you ever going to show me a rose?" As we were sitting there eating supper, our friend Susan said, "Let me show you a picture I took today of this rose. I later learned from Susan that the rosebush was planted by a World War II veteran.

After he passed away, Susan became a caregiver of the veteran's wife, and she saw that the rosebush was in bad shape, so she began putting banana peelings around the bush to help it grow. The rosebush bloomed November 29th, the same day I asked St. Therese, "Are you ever going to show me a rose?" That's the day that Susan took the picture, and there is also a wire cross in that picture. I didn't know the cross existed. I was giving a testimony at a Celebrate Recovery meeting, and as the picture was put up on the screen, I talked about the crosses in the other pictures, and the video person said, "Well, there's a cross in that picture too." Another interesting fact is that the miracle happened on April 29th. It was our anniversary, and we were beginning our 24th year of marriage. St. Therese died at the age of 24.

I still attend Celebrate Recovery, and I am still working on my recovery at 78 years of age in 2020. It is a lifelong mission. I am still involved in Celebrate Recovery as a chemical dependency leader at a Christian church where I now live in Rolla, Missouri. I believe that God has a plan for all of our lives. In Jeremiah 1:5, it says *"Before I formed you in the womb, I knew you. Before you were born, I sanctified you, and I ordained you to be a prophet of all nations."* When I think about my life and the difficult road that God has made me travel so I may have the knowledge and compassion to serve him and share Celebrate Recovery programs in jails and prisons, the verse in the Bible that has helped me the most traveling the difficult road that God has planned for me, is Isaiah 41:10 which says, *"Do not fear, for I am with you. Do not be afraid, for I am your God. I will strengthen you, I will help you, I will uphold you with my victorious right hand."*

As you can see, even in this great tragedy that happened, God has turned it into a victory.

Update on this document in the present year of 2020: My wife Judy has passed away this year of 2020, and I often think of our wonderful experience at Caney Mountain together as being one of the most beautiful experiences of our lives together.

Addie is now 13 years old. I talked to her mother Karen not very long ago, and I asked her why she was able to trust me enough to just hand Addie over to me that night after I told her the story when we were at Caney Mountain so long ago. She said she knew no one could possibly make up a story like that!

Another strange thing to confirm this miracle of recognizing Addie as the same little girl in my visions is that I had always noticed a scar on the left side of her face. That scar was present and is still present now. Karen explained that when Addie was 2 years old, many of her heart tumors (segas) went away, but they started growing on the left side of her face as angiofibromas with plaques on her forehead also seen as white patches, and she had seizure activity as well. Addie has been treated through Washington University, next to Barnes, and the seizures and other symptoms have been fairly well controlled with a drug called Afinitor since she was 6 years old. Tuberous sclerosis is not a death sentence; however, 5 to 15 victims die each year from the seizures if they are not kept under control. Karen reports that Addie is still a very happy girl and always smiles at everybody. Karen is very active in the tuberous sclerosis organization, and you may want to check out that website at: tsalliance.org. Karen also takes part in the walk-a-thon for tuberous sclerosis in Washington, D.C. every year.

Addie and her mom Karen 2019

Pray this novena and St. Therese might

send you a rose from Heaven.

Zvonimir Atletic | Shutterstock

Countless people (even Pope Francis) attest to the mysterious appearance of roses at the end of their novena in honor of St. Therese of Lisieux.

It is not very often that God will allow a visible, tangible sign that confirms a particular prayer request. Often we are left confused and not entirely certain that God heard our prayers (though sometimes we will look back and see God's hand at work regardless of a sign).

On the other hand, St. Therese of Lisieux, a Carmelite nun who lived during the late 1800s, has repeatedly been the channel through which God has confirmed countless prayer intentions.

She said before she died, "**My mission — to make God loved — will begin after my death ... I will spend my heaven doing good on earth. I will let fall a shower of roses.**"

While this bold claim can be interpreted in a spiritual way, many people believe that St. Therese has answered their prayers with a **physical rose.**

Pope Francis is one of the most well-known proponents of the **"rose novena."** According to the Catholic News Agency, Pope Francis said to journalists, "When I don't know how things are going to go, I have the custom of asking Saint Therese of the Child Jesus to take the problem into her hands and **that she send me a rose.**"

The pope reportedly will receive white roses in answer to a prayer, while others claim they receive red roses at the conclusion of their nine days of prayer.

While people might ask if there are particular "magic words" that will make the rose appear, there exists no such thing. God does not respond to prayers that are insincere and are only looking for a sign. God rewards those who pray from their heart and who are prepared to do his will, no matter what the result may be.

Those who pray the rose novena do so out of their love of God and their desire to follow the "little way" of St. Therese. She taught during her life how we should "do small things with great love." Whatever it is, even it is washing the dishes, the key is to do it with great love.

Technically the rose novena does not require a specific "formula" to invoke St. Therese's intercession, but for those who are not sure what to pray, below is the most common prayer that millions of souls have prayed over the years. Often people will pray this for a period of nine days and at the end of the nine days, a rose might appear to confirm that prayer intention. You are never guaranteed a rose, but to someone who is ready to receive God's will, anything is possible.

O Little Therese of the Child Jesus

Please pick for me a rose

from the heavenly garden

and send it to me

as a message of love.

O Little Flower of Jesus,

ask God to grant the favors

I now place with confidence

in your hands

(mention your special prayer request here).

St. Therese, help me to always believe

as you did, in God's great love for me,

so that I may imitate your "Little Way" each

day.

Amen.

Saint Thérèse of the Child Jesus

"I would never have believed it possible to suffer so much. Never! Ever! I can only explain it through the ardent desire I have to save souls..."

GOD'S PLAN FOR MY LIFE

God had a mission for me: the day the elephant grass was too green to burn, the night I thought we would bleed to death because of leeches, the day I stumbled and a sniper bullet just missed me, the day the Viet Cong general decided to take a different route, the day an injury prevented me from being ambushed along with my platoon, all tell me God had a purpose and a plan for my life.

In 2005, I started a 12-step recovery program called Celebrate Recovery at Ridgecrest Baptist Church in Springfield, Missouri. I served as a small group leader for people with chemical dependencies.

In 2007, I started Celebrate Recovery Inside, a program at the Ozark Correctional Facility (a prison) at Fordland, Missouri. We averaged from 140-160 men in attendance every week the at the Celebrate Recovery Inside step-study program, which was more in-depth, took at least six months to complete, and required total commitment and transparency. To date, more than 2000 men have now graduated from the Celebrate Recovery Inside program! Some went on to start their own Celebrate Recovery programs in the churches they were attending. Some started Celebrate Recovery programs in the prisons in which they served time. I understand that Celebrate Recovery Inside is now in every prison in the state of Missouri.

I was asked to put on a Celebrate Recovery training seminar to show people how to start a Celebrate Recovery Inside prison ministry. We had people attend from several states. I know that at least seven prison ministries were started out of that conference. In 2005, I was also asked by Victory Mission in Springfield, Missouri, to do a special recovery-themed church service on the third Sunday of the month. I did the service for 13 years until I moved to Rolla, Missouri. Right now, I serve as a small group leader for chemical dependency at a

Celebrate Recovery group in a Christian church in Rolla .

I have now been encouraged and helped by relatives, friends, and even some strangers (who miraculously showed up into my world at just the right time) to write this book in order to share my own experiences. My hope is that it will be helpful and relatable for veterans who came back from war both physically and emotionally wounded, and their families who sympathize with the trauma that has changed relationships so profoundly.

I hope those who suffer from just plain old lack of love as children, who feel broken and have no confidence, who are bruised and beaten down in so many ways, will be able to understand how to take back their right to fight for their recovery from all these evils and never give up on their ability to rise above all else to be anything they want to be.

Even though I have struggled with alcohol, anger and being mad at God for not being with my platoon when they were ambushed, God has given me another chance, and I have tried to make the best of it. My faith in God has been fully restored, and the next time I lay on my death bed, as I did that night on that jungle floor, I can say, **"Yeah, my life HAS counted for something!"**

NEVER GIVE UP!

ABOUT THE AUTHOR

ROBERT JAMES (BOB) GANNON

Bob Gannon was born August 1, 1942, and grew up in a quaint little town called Argyle, Missouri.

Bob had a serious learning disability but strongly desired to make something special out of his life, and he decided the Marine Corps could be that opportunity to do just that. He began boot camp on May 16, 1960.

In 1962, while stationed in the Philippines, he swam on the Marine team where he won the interservice championship swimming at 400 meters.

He then transferred to Camp Pendleton, California. Swimming on the Marine team and his athletic skills caused him to be selected to join Charlie Company, First Recon Battalion. (Only 1% of all the Marines are selected to go through Recon training, and about half of this select group make it through the training.)

He was sent to Vietnam, and three months into the mission, the original platoon sergeant was wounded, and Bob was then selected to replace that platoon sergeant at only 24 years of age.

He led 24 missions deep into enemy territory and was awarded the Navy Commendation medal for leadership.

In 1968, Bob was again sent back to Vietnam as a platoon sergeant; however, after five months, he was injured and sadly received a medical discharge from the Marines. Because of the two combat tours in Vietnam, he suffered posttraumatic stress syndrome and struggled for the next 25 years with alcohol, anger, nightmares, and flashbacks. In 2015, the symptoms became so severe, Bob was bordering on suicide. He prayed a novena to St. Therese (a nine-day prayer vigil), in return, she performed an amazing healing miracle. Because of childhood struggles and years of struggling with mental issues, Bob has developed a compassion for helping others in recovery programs such as:

- Developed a Gold Star service to honor families of veterans who were killed in Afghanistan and Iraq. These services total 13 during this time.

- Spent three years taking the gospel into the jail in Mt. Vernon, Missouri.
- Introduced a program called Celebrate Recovery in Fordland Prison, Fordland, Missouri. There were 140 to 160 inmates per week. Over 2000 men have graduated from this step study which takes eight months to complete. It became a model program for Celebrate Recovery in the United States. He then presented a seminar for people who wanted to take Celebrate Recovery into prisons.
- Bob spent 13 years performing the third Sunday church service at Victory Mission, Springfield, Missouri.
- Bob is currently serving as a chemical dependency leader in the Christian Church in Rolla, Missouri. He has presented his stories at eight different conference locations as well as multiple Celebrate Recovery programs.
- He is presently authoring his first book entitled <u>NEVER GIVE UP</u>.

BOB GANNON 2020

Enjoying summer on Bob's front porch, 2020

FRONT, LEFT TO RIGHT: **JOE GANNON** (son), **BOB GANNON,** AUTHOR

TIM RIELLY (husband of Trish Gannon Rielly), **ANGELA GANNON** (wife of Joe Gannon)

BACKGROUND LEFT: LINDA GALBRAITH, EDITOR

BACKGROUND MIDDLE: TRISH GANNON RIELLY *(daughter)*

Author Robert J. Gannon
About This Book

Bob's hopes are that this documentation might help others...others who came back from war with so much damage both physically and emotionally. Also to help their families understand how their loved ones seem to be a different person when they came home than when they left. So many family members suffer from the isolation effects of PTSD and feel rejected and unloved because they do not understand the symptoms of the disease, and so many times the veterans do not understand either because they have not asked for help.

There are many others who suffer from just plain old lack of love as children, who feel broken and have no confidence, who are bruised and beaten down in so many ways. The hopes are they, too, will be able to understand how to take back their right to fight for their recovery from all these evils and **never give up** on their ability to rise above all else to be anything they want to be.

Made in the USA
Monee, IL
09 March 2021

61461009R00204